VAXLIT

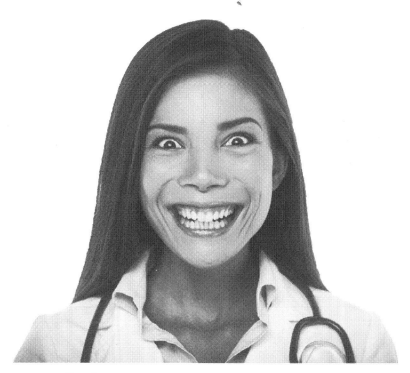

VACCINATED FROM TRUTH

THE PHARMACEUTICAL REP

VAXLIT: Vaccinated From Truth

Printed in the United States of America

ISBN: 978-0-578-37049-1

GETTR: @vaxlit
email: vaxlit@gmail.com

Acknowledgements

I want to thank TG and SS, two of the best Pharmaceutical Managers in the business. You believed in me, supported me, and gave me a chance. You kept it real and were 'old school.'

– THANK YOU.

Table of Contents

Foreword

I am a physician who has been practicing medicine for 22 years. What has gone on the last two years during COVID-19 has been complete bullshit! I have never before seen the practice of medicine and treatment of patients so compromised. I receive threatening emails from the large hospital organization I work for telling me I can't prescribe certain medications proven to help my patients. At the same time, I am coerced to highly encourage the COVID vaccine for all my patients, despite some of my patients experiencing severe reactions to the COVID vaccine. The practice of medicine is under attack.

I have known the Pharmaceutical Rep for many years. He is one of the most well-liked and trustworthy pharmaceutical representatives who has ever come into our office. In VAXLIT, The Pharmaceutical Rep takes you behind the scene and sheds light on the devious nature of the current practice of medicine related to Covid and the vaccines. I highly recommend this book. It is a must read!

Sincerely,

M.D.

PART I

—————

COVID-19 Headlines

CHAPTER 1

Significant Changes

A person who has had a documented COVID-19 infection in the past 90 days is considered the equivalent of 'fully vaccinated.'
—*NCAA* COVID-19 Medical Advisory Board (1/6/22)

I want out of this pandemic. You want out of this pandemic. We all want out. Enough already! We want things to go back to normal. We simply want to live again. Left or right, conservative or liberal, Republican or Democrat, we all have the same goal. We want to win over COVID-19. We are sick of losing to this thing. Originally, we were told the pandemic would last only two weeks. Then we thought maybe only two months. It has been two years! You know the definition of insanity: doing the same thing over and over and expecting different results. We need to try something different, because what we're doing is clearly not working.

The last two years has taken its toll physically, emotionally, and spiritually on all of us. COVID-19 is not discriminatory. We have all been impacted in one way or another. We have learned a lot over the last two years. And every day it seems we learn something new. In fact, change is the only thing that has remained a constant through it all. Some of these changes are showing just a sliver of light at the end of the tunnel. But we need to keep our eyes peeled wide open if we are to catch a glimpse of the way out.

Every day on the news we see a new headline related to COVID-19 and the vaccines. In this chapter, we are going to examine a few of the most significant changes that took place between November 2021 - February 2022. We will start with the major headlines related directly to COVID-19, the vaccines, and your health.

Lockdown Effectiveness

Johns Hopkins University meta-analysis, 2/1/22:

- Lockdowns during the first COVID-19 wave in the spring of 2020 only reduced COVID-19 mortality by 0.2% in the U.S. and Europe.

- While this meta-analysis concludes that lockdowns have had little to no public health effects, they have imposed enormous economic and social costs where they have been adopted.

- The researchers concluded, 'In consequence, lockdown policies are ill-founded and should be rejected as a pandemic policy instrument.'

Another significant change is the changes the CDC have recently made regarding quarantine time. Here are the details:

» In mid-December 2021, CDC director Rochelle Walensky decided to shorten the guidelines from a 10-day quarantine time for those infected with Covid to a 5-day quarantine time.

» Walensky said the shorter quarantine guidelines were meant to alleviate the strains on the healthcare system because so many pharmacists, doctors and nurses were being sidelined.

Let me be clear, this is a good thing, and the CDC is finally on the right track. But how did quarantine time go from two weeks, to ten days, to only five days? Did the science of the disease change? Did our understanding of transmission change?

This change had everything to do with our economy and nothing to do with protecting our citizens. **If lockdowns and mandates were truly about our safety then every illegal immigrant who crossed our Southern border would have to be vaccinated.** This is NOT happening. But in NYC, residents are required to show proof of vaccination before getting even a burger and fries. Something doesn't add up? Could this change have to do with the fact that in January 2022 America hit its worse inflation rate in forty years? This change was about politics, not your health.

If you thought lockdown and quarantine initiatives were bad in the US, check out China's:

- Liu Guozhong, the party chief of Shaanxi Province in China, instructed local Xi'an capital officials to "tap into the wartime spirit and quarantine anyone at risk without a moment of delay."

- People in this Chinese province are being hauled away as prisoners to Covid quarantine camps or literally being locked down behind metal doors barring them exit from their own residential compounds.

- This sounds like Nazi Germany and should scare the hell out of us.

    o   Why did we send athletes to China to compete in the Olympics?

Big Pharma: Pfizer & *Pfizermectin*

Pfizer is top of mind when most people think of the pharmaceutical industry, especially related to COVID-19 vaccines. Pfizer truly puts the *big* in Big Pharma. They are definitely the big boys on the block:

- Pfizer's stock price has soared +34.77% from July 2021 to January 2022.

- 2/1/22 – Pfizer is now seeking COVID vaccine approval in the United States for infants 6 months old and older.

  o The U.S. is the only place in the world pushing Covid vaccines on **infants**.

- Pfizer initially stated their Covid vaccine would offer 99% protection. Why isn't mainstream media holding them accountable for this blatant lie?

We all know Pfizer manufactures the most widely used COVID-19 vaccine in the world. But did you also know on December 22, 2021 the FDA approved Pfizer's oral antiviral drug, Paxlovid, to treat Covid. Interesting facts regarding this pill:

- » The FDA fact sheet states Paxlovid can cause severe or life-threatening reactions when used in conjunction with many other common medications.

- » In November 2021, the Biden administration purchased ten million courses of the new antiviral. Guess how much the price tag was: $5 billion dollars. (I can see Dr. Evil from *Austin Powers* right now!)

» 30 million of a planned 80 million treatment courses of Paxlovid will be available in the first six months of 2022.

Pfizer should have really named Paxlovid, *Pfizermectin.* Their new antiviral is biosimilar to Merck's old anti-viral drug ivermectin which won the **Nobel Prize for Medicine** in 2015 for its outstanding anti-viral treatment in HUMANS. CNN and other outlets spread outrageous misinformation that ivermectin was only intended for horses and livestock. What's important to know is that ivermectin is off patent, so drug companies make no money on it, thus the need for a "new" one.

Even more alarming, a number of physicians I call on showed me emails they received from the large HCOs (health care organizations) they work for. These emails directly threaten doctors with their jobs if they prescribe ivermectin, even though ivermectin is helping their patients recover from Covid. I guarantee you Pfizer's Paxlovid, (*Pfizermectin*), won't be suppressed by the government and large HCOs. But instead, your physician group will be incentivized to write it.

Ivermectin
Let's briefly talk about ivermectin while we are on the subject. After all, it elicits quite a reaction if you tell someone who only watches CNN that you are using it to treat COVID-19. But before you judge, lets' look at the facts. Ivermectin is on the World Health Organization's (WHO) coveted List of Essential Medicines, and is approved by the FDA. And just to be crystal clear here, we are talking about humans, not animals. It's one of the most effective and safest drugs prescribed over the last 30 years. Maybe that's why it won the Nobel Prize for Medicine in 2015. A couple data points about ivermectin/COVID-19 vaccines from the FDA and CDC in VAERS:

7

» From 1996 - 2021 there have only been 15 deaths per year associated with ivermectin use.

» In 13 months, there have been 20,175 deaths per year associated with the COVID-19 vaccines.

   o 30% of these deaths occurred within the first 2 days after taking the vaccine. (This statistic indicates causality.)

To give fair balance, ivermectin is used off label to treat COVID-19. But every drug out there is basically used off label by your doctor for one thing or another. Just ask him or her.

The whole banning of ivermectin, which we will get into in greater detail later, is really all about money. Big Pharma and the government aren't really looking out for your health by banning the use of ivermectin. If this whole thing was really about our health and safety, it's worth repeating, then every illegal immigrant who crossed our Southern border would be getting vaccinated. But they are not. Following the money trail can be extremely disheartening, especially when the quality of your healthcare is negatively affected.

Natural Immunity vs. Vaccinated Immunity

"A person who has had a documented COVID-19 infection in the past 90 days is considered the equivalent of 'fully vaccinated.'"- *NCAA* COVID-19 Medical Advisory Board (1/6/21).

The NCAA, the nation's largest collegiate sports organization, is now recognizing natural immunity is equivalent to vaccinated immunity. The NCAA states its latest guidance "was developed in consultation with the NCAA COVID-19 Medical Advisory Group, American

Medical Society for Sports Medicine Working Group, and Autonomy 5 Medical Advisory Group and takes into consideration available recommendation from the CDC." The equivalency of vaccinated immunity and natural immunity is a seismic shift to what we were all previously told. And the fact there are no negative side effects with natural immunity is a game-changer:

- Is natural immunity now legit? If so, this changes everything.

- Why isn't natural immunity being talked about on <u>every</u> news outlet?

- This headline could mean we are closer to an endemic than a pandemic.

Denmark came out with a study in January 2022 stating the unvaccinated are handling Omicron better than the vaccinated due to the unvaccinated having a higher level of natural immunity. (To give this study fair balance, it has not yet been peer reviewed, but the data looks promising.)

Covid vaccines are shown to **reduce**, not boost, antibodies. A recent University of Oxford study showed a lower level of antibodies against Omicron is actually triggered by getting the vaccine. Oxford Study:

» The study showed further evidence there is a "substantial fall" in neutralizing antibodies, which will likely lead to an increased breakthrough of Covid infections.

» This will ultimately lead to a surge in Covid cases in the winter of 2021/2022.

Vaccine Safety (VAERS)

The Vaccine Adverse Event Reporting System (VAERS) is a United States program for vaccine safety, co-managed by the U.S. Centers for Disease Control and Prevention (CDC) and the Food and Drug Administration (FDA). VAERS is a post-marketing surveillance program, collecting information about adverse events related to vaccines. VAERS is where doctors, hospital administrators, nurses, etc. go to report side effects related to vaccines. When you read the statistics below, remember this is government run. This is not some right-wing medical organization. I say this because when you see the data you might be tempted to think it's "misinformation" by some right-wing conspirator:

VAERS data as of January 2022:

* COVID-19 vaccines account for 3X more deaths than ALL other vaccines combined over the last thirty years.

* VAERS COVID-19 vaccine data as of January 7, 2022:
  » 21,745 deaths
  » 25,773 cases of myocarditis/pericarditis
  » 37,973 permanently disabled
  » 3,594 miscarriages

* Harvard study: Data revealed less than 1% of all adverse incidents are actually reported to VAERS.
  » VAERS data is just scratching the surface on adverse events.

If these GOVERNMENT, both CDC and FDA, statistics don't get you questioning the safety of the vaccines then you are not following the science but a false, yet very powerful, narrative that you are being fed every night on CNN.

COVID-19/Comorbidities

While we are on the subject of the CDC and FDA, let's check in with what CDC director Rochelle Walensky recently said during a *Good Morning America* interview on 1/7/2022:

"The overwhelming number of COVID deaths, over 75%, occurred in people who had at least four comorbidities. So really, these are people who were unwell to begin with."

Let that soak in for a second. The director of the CDC is saying over 75% of people who died from COVID were already sick, or in her exact words, "unwell to begin with." So, the question needs to be asked; are people dying **from** COVID or **with** COVID. She states that the majority of COVID-19 deaths can't actually be classified as "COVID-19 deaths." Why is the news not shouting this from the rooftops? Why isn't mainstream media jumping on this headline? People dying from comorbidities, not Covid, is a huge deal.

Omicron

Let's hear what Pfizer CEO, Albert Bourla, recently said about COVID vaccines and Omicron:

In an interview on 1/10/2022 at JP Morgan's Healthcare Conference, Bourla said this, "The two doses, they're not enough for Omicron. We have seen with a second dose very clearly that the first thing that we lost was the protection against infections."

The CEO of Pfizer is telling us the vaccines don't work on Omicron. Let me say that again, **THE CEO OF PFIZER TOLD US THE VACCINES ARE NOT ENOUGH!** If we are all being force-fed the ideology that we all need to get the vaccine and then a booster regardless of whether they actually work or not, what is really going on here?

The ubiquitous permeation of Omicron across the entire globe is clear evidence the Pfizer CEO is correct. Yet, we are still being mandated to take a vaccine which is clearly not working. How do we reconcile this gross inconsistency? The vaccine may have helped a little with the initial strain of COVID-19, but it is clearly not effective against other strains like Omicron.

Dr. Robert Malone, inventor of mRNA technology which the vaccines are founded upon, said recently, "Omicron could be a gift to us all. Almost all of us are going to get it and it will produce robust natural immunity." Omicron is highly transmissible, and the vaccines won't be able to stop it. However, Dr. Malone urges people to stay calm because there will be few, if any, deaths due to Omicron.

Vaccinated vs. Unvaccinated

Cancer specialist, Dr. Ryan Cole said, "It's a pathophysiological lie that this is a pandemic of the unvaccinated" Dr. Cole's qualifications:

- o Dr. Cole is certified by the American Board of Pathology as a clinical and anatomic pathologist, a doctor who examines tissue from a biopsy to look for cancer. He has operated a lab, Cole Diagnostics, for nearly 20 years as a pathologist.

- o If this was a pandemic of the unvaccinated, the vaccinated wouldn't be getting sick post vaccination. But they most certainly do. Furthermore, they wouldn't be able to spread the disease. But they most certainly do.

- o Mainstream media is trying to paint Dr. Cole as some rogue Cancer specialist with some hidden agenda because he has prescribed ivermectin and hydroxychloroquine.

○ Dr. Cole makes no money prescribing these generic medications. And even more importantly, he makes no money prescribing the vaccines. So, who is really spewing the misinformation here?

Covid is spread by the unvaccinated **and** vaccinated alike. And we now know vaccination does not prevent you from getting Covid. In fact, some data, like the studies mentioned above, demonstrate that getting vaccinated can actually weaken your immune system and prevent you from developing hearty antibodies. From the new data recently published about transmissibility, we now know Biden was dead wrong when he said, "This is a pandemic of the unvaccinated."

COVID-19/Border Crisis

Here are a couple statistics regarding the border crisis. And this most certainly relates to being VAXLIT since all illegal immigrants coming into our country are **unvaccinated**. If you are mad at the unvaccinated people in our country, you should be livid at the current administration for letting millions of people into our country unvaccinated. Talk about a health risk! If one upsets you and not the other, you have been taken for a ride. Anyway, here's a recent immigration statistic:

On December 9, 2021, Yuma, Arizona, mayor Douglas Nicholls declared a state of emergency due to the number of illegal immigrants flooding in from Mexico. Arizona had more than 21,000 illegal border crossers arrested in the month of October **alone**. As of December 2021, the total year-to-date illegals surged to 115,000.

Politicized Pandemic

Biden said repeatedly during his campaign that he would, "Shut down the virus, not the country." He then enacted federal control and power by dictating companies with one hundred or more employees mandate vaccination:

-On Wednesday, December 29, 2021, in an interview with ABC's David Muir, Biden admitted the federal government can't control Omicron, "Nobody saw it coming, nobody in the whole world." Never mind every virologist with half a brain saw many less potent but more transmissible strains of Covid coming. That's what viruses do; they mutate!

-On Tuesday, December 28, 2021, Biden told the leaders of twenty-five states, "Look, there is no federal solution. This gets solved at a state level." This is the exact opposite approach of mandating vaccinations on a federal level. Florida governor Ron DeSantis immediately fired back by demanding Biden scrap his "useless" vaccine mandates.

-Biden's current verbiage shifts responsibility off of the federal government and onto the governors of each state. As most doctors already knew, you can't "mandate" a virus from spreading!

Anthony Fauci, who is a politician with a medical degree, not the other way around, is starting to be found out. What once was considered sheer conspiracy theory regarding Fauci being intricately involved with the Wuhan lab's gain of function experiments is starting to show itself as reality. Read Robert F. Kennedy Jr.'s book, *The Real Anthony Fauci*, to get the facts on Fauci. And to be clear, this book is not a right versus left narrative. Kennedy is obviously a Democrat firmly embedded on the left:

- ○ If only a fraction of Kennedy's book is true, Fauci will wind up in prison or receive the ultimate injection –lethal injection.
- ○ If Kennedy's book is not true, Kennedy will wind up in prison for libel.

Cleveland Clinic/Mandates

In December of 2021, many prominent healthcare organizations dropped the vaccine mandate due to critical healthcare staffing shortages.

-The Cleveland Clinic is just one example of a major HCO that has changed their policy regarding the vaccine mandate.

In December 2021, four states called in the National Guard to help with a nationwide healthcare staffing *crisis*. (Wait, I'm allowed to say *crisis* here, right? Yeah, I am. It was the border issue that you weren't allowed to make reference to the word *crisis*.)

CNN & Mainstream Media

Mainstream media has played a critical role in the pandemic. Those on the right think mainstream media is dishonest and spewing misinformation. Those on the left think anything mainstream media says is fact. There is a great divide in our country due to this information war. Below are the latest headlines related to CNN, Twitter, and Spotify:

CNN

> 2/2/2022, CNN's President, Jeff Zucker, resigns abruptly. (The shit is really starting to hit the fan at CNN! But this is only the beginning.)

At the time I began this book, Chris Cuomo just got fired from CNN for shady dealings with his disgraced brother. Now CNN producer Rick Saleeby of *The Lead with Jake Tapper* has resigned because he is under criminal investigation involving "potential juvenile victims." There are legitimate reasons for CNN's sharp decline in ratings over the last year:

- This is the second CNN producer to resign for "inducing minors for sex." CNN is not only dishonest newscasters; it also seems to be a den of pedophiles.

- If you are still watching CNN, you deserve to be deceived.

CNN just named their "2021 CEO of the Year." Guess who it was? None other than Pfizer's CEO, Albert Bourla. No surprise here:

- Does the picture become a little clearer why CNN can't take any "misinformation" stating the vaccines actually may have some problems? Talk about a conflict of interest.

Twitter

As of January 18, 2022, Twitter stock has plummeted -45.10 percent over the last six months. Here's what's gone down in January 2022 on Twitter:

> -Twitter permanently banned Dr. Robert Malone, the inventor of mRNA technology and one of the top virologists in the world.

-Joe Rogan switched from Twitter to GETTR and took over one million followers with him.

Spotify

- Neil Young told Spotify to get rid of the Joe Rogan podcast with Dr. Robert Malone or get rid of his music. (BTW- Over 50 million viewers watched the podcast.) Spotify removed Neil Young. Neil Young is so woke he actually cancelled himself!

- Neil Young is financially tied to Pfizer. Big pharma's big boy owns Neil and his music. On January 6, 2021, Mr. Young sold half of his catalogue to Merck Mercuriadis' Hipgnosis Song Management company:
  - Later in 2021 Hipgnosis merged with Blackstone in a USD$1Billion dollar deal.
  - A month before the merger Blackstone announced they appointed Pfizer's former Chairman and CEO Jeffrey B Kindler as the company's Senior Advisor.

Even with all the recent headlines related to COVID-19 and the vaccines, we are still constantly being told the vaccines are safe and effective. We are literally being told that what we are seeing and hearing isn't real. It reminds me of the gaslighting that took place at the end of the now infamous NASCAR race. NBC sports reporter, Kelli Stavast, told us the crowd was chanting, "Let's Go Brandon." We could clearly hear they were chanting something entirely different! The rest is history. Mainstream media was caught red-handed gaslighting the American people. Now we are being gaslit about the safety and efficacy of the COVID vaccines. Actually, we are being more than gaslit, we are being *VAXLIT*.

How is COVID-19 being played out in your doctor's office? How do the politics of Big Pharma, Big Government, and Big Tech affect you and your family's healthcare? And furthermore, how have we gotten to this place of two separate "realities" in our culture? A bipolar neurosis has swept over our country's landscape. Our society is severely fractured and something's got to give. Both sides of the aisle will agree on this.

I am not claiming to have all the answers. But Big Pharma, Big Government, and Big Tech obviously don't have them either. The diabolical thing here is they are claiming to have *the* one answer. And that is to vaccinate everyone, including children AND infants. But this is clearly not working; Omicron is evident of that. It is ripping through the world's entire population, vaccinated or not.

I had Omicron myself. I did what my doctor recommended, which is take therapeutics like ivermectin, vitamins, and a diluted nasal rinse of povidone iodine. I had a fever for a couple of days and a bad head cold for a week. But I recovered, without being vaccinated. Remember, the Pfizer CEO said the vaccines don't work against Omicron, not me.

What we need is healthy debate and robust discussion among the top virologists and physicians in the world about what is working and what's not. It's time to ditch the scientific oligarchy of Mr. Science himself, Anthony Fauci. It's time to listen to a plethora of virologists who have differing opinions. Not just the ones Joe Biden or CNN have pimped out. I feel extremely blessed to be in a position to hear both sides of this debate every single day out in the field as a pharmaceutical rep.

Only as we allow and relish in healthy debate, versus squelching any negative Covid data and discussion, will we come out the other side with truth. And only after we discover truth will there be a successful way forward. Until then we will be walking around in darkness with our eyes wide shut. Until we know the truth, we won't be free. As Jesus said, "Then you will know the truth, and the truth will set you free" (John 8:32 NIV).

If you want to know the truth about Big Pharma, doctors, and the vaccine, then take up and read. However, if you want to remain in the land of make-believe and unicorns, then grab a bag of popcorn, turn on CNN/Chris Cuomo, and enjoy the show. (Oh, I forgot, Chris Cuomo was fired for being dishonest.) Maybe it's time for some reality. Maybe it's time for healthy debate and truthful talk versus a one-size-fits-all narrative propagated by Big Pharma, Big Government, and Mainstream Media. Let's take a closer look.

PART II

———

Gaslighting…Gaslit…*VAXLIT*

CHAPTER 2

A Pharmaceutical Rep

You have the best relationships with doctors, nurses, and staff I have ever seen.

—Regional Sales Manager; Big Pharma

The quote above is one of the best compliments I have ever received in seventeen years as a pharmaceutical sales representative. It came from a higher-up in the Big Pharma company I work for. He spent the entire day with me calling on my accounts. He could clearly see I had developed great relationships with the doctors I call on.

The importance of the compliment he gave me is simply to give context as to what type of relationships I have with the doctors in my territory. This is extremely important information to know before I tell you what you are about to hear. You see, if you don't trust someone, you don't tell them truthful things about very sensitive issues. However, if you do develop a trusting relationship, then a free flow of honest communication is the norm. Being truthful with one another is simply a natural result of a trusting relationship. And that is exactly what I have with many of my physicians.

I have been in the pharmaceutical industry for seventeen years. My entire career has been working for one of the largest Big Pharma companies in the world. I have seen and heard a lot from the doctors I have called on during my seventeen-year career. And the last couple of years during Covid have been absolutely remarkable, or reprehensible, depending on how you look at it.

Some of my closest friends are the physicians who I have called on for many years. I mean really close friends. Like having them over for Thanksgiving dinner, praying together for their kids, attending their weddings, and the list goes on. The point is, I know many of the doctors in my territory very, very well.

What you are about to hear comes from things I see and hear every single day from doctors who are my friends. But not only that, since I work for Big Pharma, I am deeply embedded in the politics of Big Pharma and understand how a pharmaceutical company operates. I see the trickle-down effects of Big Pharma policy filter all the way down into your doctor's office. I see firsthand how this impacts the quality of your healthcare.

To give you a little more context into who I am and what I see, it is fair I share more than just what I do for a living. My faith plays a huge role in my life. My relationship with God is front and center. I minored in Biblical Studies at the Christian University I attended. And I am currently working on a graduate degree in Biblical Studies. I thoroughly enjoy studying Biblical principles and how the implementation of those principles can positively impact our lives.

I also am a husband and father. I absolutely love my wife and kids. And I believe investing time into those relationships to be a high calling. My relationship with God, myself, and my family are the most important things in my life. I try and practice a healthy work-life balance so I can effectively live out my beliefs. Sometimes I am successful, sometimes I'm not.

At the outset, I also want to share a little about the Big Pharma company I work for. I have been with this company for the entirety of my seventeen years in pharmaceuticals. My company has served and helped a multitude of patients over the years. We truly have marketed some amazing life changing medications that have helped not only the general public, but also some of my closest friends and family members. I am proud of the choices and integrity my company has displayed in putting patients first. For my company, putting patients first hasn't just been a nice little catch-phrase, but an actual corporate practice. It has been a great place to work. That is why I have stayed with the company for so long, despite getting calls every year from multiple headhunters with other lucrative opportunities. However, just like thousands of other companies across the globe, my company has truly lost their way dealing effectively with COVID-19 and the vaccine mandates.

My company is one of the Big Pharma giants who manufacture the COVID-19 vaccine. Because of this, I am remaining anonymous at the time of this writing. People get offended when you call their baby ugly. And Big Pharma is certainly no exception. Right now the First Amendment is not being upheld when people speak out against the Covid vaccines and mandates. Hopefully in a couple months you can speak out without fear of losing your job. Things are starting to slowly change, but we are not there yet. I am protecting both myself and the doctors I call on by remaining anonymous at this time.

I am going to share with you what I see and hear from doctors, nurses, and Big Pharma related to the pandemic, COVID-19, and the vaccines. What I am about to share with you are facts. These are real-life events.

These are not fake stories on right or left news media outlets, but real events that take place in my doctors' offices every single day. This is an exclusive look at the innermost workings of Big Pharma, physicians, and the COVID-19 vaccines. Let's begin to take a peek behind the curtain.

CHAPTER 3

The Problem of the Pandemic

You're an idiot if you *don't* get the vaccine. —**Doctor A**

You're an idiot if you *do* get the vaccine. —**Doctor B**

As a pharmaceutical representative with a lot of close doctor friends, I walk into a large family practice, and one doctor tells me his patients are idiots if they *don't* get vaccinated. Then, five minutes later, I walk down the hall and talk to his partner in the same practice, and she tells me the exact opposite. She says her patients that *do* get the vaccine are idiots because they are not following the science. What's a patient to do? What are you and I to do?

Here's the kicker: both doctors are my good friends. I have been to each of their homes for dinners and parties, and they have been to mine. I have golfed, played tennis, gone boating, etc. with each of these friends, who also happen to be doctors. Our entire families get together just to hang out. Both work in the same city, in the very same practice, with the same degree: MD. And both of these physicians are extremely intelligent and well-rounded individuals.

Here's where it gets confusing. Two doctors in the very same city, in the very same practice, and with the same medical license have extremely opposing views regarding the Covid vaccine and mandate. One is all in on the Covid vaccine and mandate, and the other is calling BS on the entire thing. But these completely differing opinions can be a great thing, **if** we embrace the debate. These differences can turn into a healthy discussion about science, patients, and what doctors are seeing every single day. This robust debate about COVID-19 and the vaccines can turn out to be enlightening for us all. But only **if** we let it.

I hear this two-sided debate every day out in the field calling on my physicians. Doctors, nurses, and staff alike are severely divided when it comes to the Covid vaccine. Healthy debate and robust conversation are how doctors and healthcare policy makers have traditionally made decisions related to your healthcare. Constructive dialogue is part of the true scientific model. Asking difficult questions, back-and-forth debate, and a quest for truth is historically how medical policy gets made. Policy is not perfected in a vacuum, but with a group of physicians, researchers, and scientists. A consortium of the best and brightest in a particular field of medicine come together to find truth and make appropriate protocols for the health and well-being of society. And the harder the medical problem is, the more questions, forums, and healthy debate is needed in order to come to the best, safest, and most logical way forward for patients. Debate, critique, and constructive criticism among physicians in order to uncover scientific truth and implement best practices are not only allowed, but highly encouraged.

Here's the problem with the pandemic. Healthy and robust debate between a group of physicians, researchers, and scientists is not happening. There's not a conglomerate of the top virologists in the world coming together to hash things out for the good of society. There's not a group of physicians who have opposing views about the spread of Covid, the efficacy of the vaccines, and the safety of the vaccines who are sitting in the same room together arguing for your health.

Not only is this not happening amongst top physicians, instead it's actually being discouraged. And we are all paying a high price for it. We are suffering in many ways because of the lack of healthy debate amongst physicians and policy makers. Whether it be our deteriorating physical health, our lack of emotional/mental well-being, our children's education in disarray, or our communities on the brink of collapse, how we have dealt with Covid has taken its toll on all of us. Let me be clear, it's not primarily Covid that has us in a state of misery. But it's *how* we have dealt with it that has us running amuck.

The goal is to beat Covid and get out of this damn pandemic, right? I know I am sick of it, and you are too. Your goal and mine are the health and well-being of our families. We want our children safe and able to get back to normal. We want them to be able to go out and play with friends, compete in sporting events and extra-curricular activities. We want some normalcy back in our own lives as well. In our work and social interactions, we want things to go back to normal. We want our communities and society to have some semblance of cohesiveness again. We all want to start living again. And we all are sick of living in fear! Take a poll of twenty people you know, and we all have these same goals. But why are we so divided?

These goals are mine and yours. And they are good goals. Good for ourselves, our families, and our society. So, what's the problem here? Well, to start, the problem is not everyone shares these same goals. But, being the good-natured people we are, we assume everyone wants to get out of the pandemic and come up with solutions that really work so we can get back to life as we knew it. But if our goals are the health and well-being of our families and wanting to put this pandemic behind us, while at the same time the goals of others are money, power, and control regardless of our health and well-being, then true solutions for our health and well-being that would end the pandemic will be suppressed and denied if those same solutions do not grant others the money, power, and control they are so desperately seeking. And if true solutions to ending the pandemic are in direct conflict with the goals of others to make money and gain power, then all hell will break lose. And that is exactly what has happened.

There is a horrible symptom to this conflict. And it's the main problem behind the pandemic: **Big Pharma, Big Government, and Big Tech are NOT allowing ANY open or honest debate regarding vaccine safety and efficacy.** In fact, they are suppressing any truth that threatens their "reality." (Thus, the extreme censorship on Twitter, YouTube, and the like.) And why wouldn't they? Truth would certainly be stifled and suppressed at all costs if it threatens the prospect of unfathomable amounts of money, power, and control. Remember, not everyone's goals are the same. Your goal and mine are for truth leading to the pandemic's end, an endemic. But if everyone's goal is not truth leading to an endemic, the pandemic will be untruthfully perpetuated.

A healthy debate and constructive arguments among the top virologists in the world could easily help us get to truth. We then could develop solutions that truly work to end the pandemic. We would all be on the same page, regardless of the solution. Vaccine or no vaccine. Therapeutics or no therapeutics. Monoclonal antibodies or no monoclonal antibodies. Vitamins or no vitamins. It wouldn't matter what the solution was as long as it worked. If real data revealed you needed to rub tea leaves all over your body and that proved effective, then I'd do it. And so would you. It wouldn't matter who came up with the solution, as long as it truly worked.

Physicians I know personally are being silenced if they have working solutions other than vaccines for beating Covid. Furthermore, any virologist, even if he or she has spent their entire career developing safe and effective vaccines, is being silenced if they dare even hint at the fact something could be wrong with these vaccines. Even if the actual **physician himself** who invented the technology behind the Covid vaccines reports data showing the vaccines are ineffective and dangerous, even he is being silenced. (By the way, this physician is also a Democrat **and** has been vaccinated!) And of course, he would be silenced because he and others like him would be the ultimate threat to a very powerful and diabolical narrative.

This kind of repression of truth and lack of an open forum to talk about the hard data related to Covid and the vaccines is absolutely terrifying. If you don't really know the truth is being suppressed, it most certainly is—and at a level that's mind-blowing. From personal real-life interactions I have every day with the physicians I call on, I will show you how widespread this suppression really is. If you, me, physicians I call on, or even some of the top virologists in the world don't follow this one-size-fits-all narrative that the vaccines are safe, effective, and the only treatment option, then you will be silenced, lose your job, and be labeled a domestic threat.

The problem behind this narrative is Big Money and corrupt power are driving it, not science. Follow the money trail, and the false narrative will become crystal clear. The stakes right now are high; they've never been higher. The search for truth amidst so many voices is daunting. The need for constructive and healthy two-sided debate has never been so needed.

Over the last two years thousands of companies, within the pharmaceutical industry and outside, have lost their way in terms of dealing effectively with COVID-19. Companies, school systems, government agencies, and a host of other entities are not following the **real** science related to COVID vaccine safety and efficacy. Instead, they are following a dictatorlike narrative forcing everyone to get vaccinated. Old, young, healthy, unhealthy, people with comorbidities, people without comorbidities, children, and now even infants. A one-size-fits-all vaccine dictate has been shamelessly shoved on us all.

I will give you the other side of the debate which I see firsthand every day out in the field from real doctors treating real patients. This is the side of the story you don't hear on your nightly news, press conferences coming out of the White House, or even from the CDC and FDA. I will give you an inside look as a pharmaceutical representative of seventeen years working for Big Pharma. I am not some disgruntled former employee of a Big Pharma company. I actually enjoy my work and respect my company, although this respect has waned tremendously over the last couple of years. Therefore, I don't have any ax to grind. But the truth needs to come out. People's lives and livelihoods are at stake here. And the corruption runs deep, really deep!

Having built solid relational capital with my physicians over the years has enabled me to hear the true other side of the story. When a good percentage of my doctors are sharing a completely different narrative than what you see on CNN, it makes you question who is actually spewing misinformation. When a doctor invites me to come into his or her office and close the door behind me so they can share with me the real deal behind Covid and the vaccines, I am all ears.

I am simply a pharmaceutical representative, a drug rep. I have been in the same territory for seventeen years. And in that time, I have developed close-knit friendships with many of the physicians I have called on. My perspective is from the frontline. I hear firsthand from doctors who care deeply about their patients. Behind closed doors, they share private stories related to the vaccine, side effects, and their patients. I go home each night absolutely shocked at what I see and hear from the doctors, nurses, and staff that I call on. These are real events and true patient stories. The information I am about to share with you comes from doctors who are battling to keep their integrity amidst mass pressure from the eye of the pandemic's storm. This is not misinformation; it is true. And you can do with it what you want.

CHAPTER 4

Second Opinion

The Covid vaccines are leaky and dangerous.
—Vaccinated Democrat who Invented mRNA Technology:
Dr. Robert Malone

I severely hurt my wrist three years ago. So much so it swelled up like a summer squash. I couldn't move it for a few weeks and the swelling really didn't go down. Not a good sign. So, I went to one of the most well-respected wrist surgeons in the area. He told me I would definitely need surgery. Furthermore, he said the sooner the better. I had to schedule surgery with his assistant before leaving his office. I took his advice and planned for surgery. However, I wanted a second opinion just to make sure. I scheduled an appointment with the other most respected wrist surgeon in town. These two were the top guys. Both had great reviews and all my doctor friends recommended either one of the two surgeons if you had wrist issues.

I went to the second doctor and he told me he would not recommend surgery. He said this was an extremely intricate surgery with just ok outcomes. He spent more time with me than the first surgeon. And I had a much better feel with this surgeon than the first. The clincher for me was when he said, "If you were my brother, I wouldn't recommend this surgery."

I am so glad I got a second opinion. I did not get the surgery. My wrist healed up in the next couple months with rest and physical therapy. I was back to almost one hundred percent within three to four months. I will have a minor twinge from time to time, but ninety nine percent of the time there is absolutely no issue with my wrist.

This chapter is devoted to getting a second opinion. Who are the top doctors in the field of virology? And what are they saying? Let's pretend like Dr. Fauci, working in the government run hospital is the first doctor we went to see for COVID-19 treatment. But two years later we are still sick and the treatment is not working. Let's go get a second opinion. Let's take a look at a few of the top physicians and hospital organizations in the world and see what they are saying about COVID vaccines and the ongoing debate of how we can best treat COVID-19.

At the outset, I want to give context regarding the first physician we will look at. He is a Democrat **and** has been vaccinated. So, if you are on the left, be assured this top virologist in the world is NOT a Trump supporter. You can actually listen to what he says despite mainstream media trying to silence him. Again, Dr. Robert Malone is a Democrat who got the COVID-19 vaccine.

Inventor of mRNA Technology: Dr. Robert Malone

One of the physicians on the other side of this debate is Dr. Robert Malone. He is the doctor who invented, let me say that again, he *invented* the mRNA technology that both the Pfizer and Moderna vaccines are founded upon. Dr. Robert Malone's résumé is pretty impressive to say the least. Below are just a few highlights from his storied career as a leader and pioneer in the field of virology and vaccine development:

He developed the core technology platform that mRNA technology is founded upon. (Pfizer and Moderna use this mRNA technology for their COVID-19 vaccines.)

- He has spent the last thirty years developing safe and effective vaccines for society.

- He has a long history of published peer-reviewed literature related to vaccine development and delivery.

- He has developed numerous medical/vaccine-related patents.

- He is **pro-vaccine**.

Dr. Robert Malone has spent his entire career developing vaccines to help and serve humanity. Despite what you may have heard on CNN, he is NOT anti-vaccine. He is one of the most pro-vaccine physicians on the face of the earth. Yet he has openly called out the COVID-19 vaccines as "leaky and dangerous." He said this because the vaccines wear out in six months and the side effects are harming people. With the mass push now for boosters, we see his claim of "leakiness" as legitimate, not misinformation. We are also hearing more and more fallout, like blood clots and myocarditis, that are wreaking havoc on many patients who received the COVID vaccine.

Dr. Malone has obviously taken a lot of heat from mainstream media because he is being honest about the flaws and pitfalls of mRNA vaccines. If you've never heard his name, you have been living under a rock or never turn off CNN. He is reporting the negative safety and efficacy data post-vaccine rollout. The data and science simply don't line up with the false narrative that Covid vaccines are safe, effective, and everyone, including children, should be taking them. He is not on board with the mandates, so he is being maligned and silenced.

Twitter just permanently banned Dr. Malone, one of the top virologists in the world and inventor of mRNA vaccines, for saying the vaccines are "toxic and can cause birth defects." That would be like banning Michael Jordan from giving basketball advice or Tiger Woods from giving golf tips. What happened to healthy debate amongst physicians to arrive at truth in order to implement appropriate protocols? What happened to free speech?

World-Renowned Cardiologist: Dr. Peter McCullough

Another one of these top physicians known around the globe is Dallas cardiologist Dr. Peter McCullough. He is not just a doctor, but at the top of the doctor food chain, a cardiologist. Here are some facts about Dr. McCullough:

- He is a nationally recognized and board-certified cardiologist.

- He was vice chief of internal medicine at Baylor University Medical Center and a professor at Texas A&M University.

- He is editor-in-chief of the journal *Reviews in Cardiovascular Medicine.*

- He is one of the most peer-reviewed published cardiologists in the entire world.

Dr. Peter McCullough has challenged the way the US health care system is treating COVID-19 patients. And he has taken some heat for standing his ground. This renowned doctor from Baylor University Medical Center in Dallas is questioning why doctors have failed to come up with an official treatment protocol for COVID-19. He is challenging the federal government's push for experimental vaccines versus affordable COVID-19 treatments already currently available.

Dr. McCullough has argued that in other countries, doctors have encountered success in using affordable COVID-19 treatments such as hydroxychloroquine and ivermectin. However, in the US, these two drugs have been banned for treatment of COVID-19 in favor of more costly experimental vaccines. He has developed inexpensive early treatment protocols for Covid that work more effectively than the vaccines and without the serious side effects.

The Cleveland Clinic

And finally, there is the Cleveland Clinic, one of the most respected and trusted health care organizations in the world. Their name says it all. What are they saying about the vaccine? What current Covid vaccine policies do they have in place?

- In June 2021, a Cleveland Clinic study finds natural Covid immunity better than fully vaccinated immunity. Here were three conclusions of this study:
  - There is no reason to vaccinate those who have been previously infected.

  - Fully vaccinated people are still getting Covid and adverse reactions. (Fast-forward six months, and it is now common knowledge and accepted in the medical community that vaccinated people can transmit the virus.)

  - Previously infected people with Covid were less likely to be reinfected than fully vaccinated individuals who never had the virus.

And more recently, on December 2, 2021, the Cleveland Clinic has reversed their employee COVID-19 vaccination mandate:

- ○ Cleveland Clinic and University Hospitals have reversed their employee COVID-19 vaccination mandates and will allow unvaccinated caregivers to keep their jobs.

- ○ Both Cleveland Clinic and UH previously announced they would comply with the new federal rule that requires health care facilities to mandate vaccinations or risk losing their CMS—Centers for Medicare and Medicaid Services **funding**. (It's all about the Benjamins.)

- ○ In a recent statement, UH officials say they changed course "in light of the federal court injunction issued November 30 that temporarily blocks CMS from enforcing the mandate."

- ○ "Come January 4, unless there is further legal action, caregivers may continue to provide patient care services regardless of their vaccination status," UH officials said in a statement.

Nobel Prize Winner: Dr. Luc Antoine Montagnier

Bonus: The two physicians listed above and the Cleveland Clinic all hail from America. Let's be fair and look at a well-known doctor from another country. How about the guy who discovered the AIDS virus in 1983? He also won the Nobel Prize in Medicine on October 6, 2008, for this discovery. He was and is a pretty big deal in the medical community.

This is French virologist Luc Antoine Montagnier. Along with other physicians like Dr. Robert Malone and Dr. Peter McCullough, he has spoken out openly about the dangers of the COVID-19 vaccine. Some of his videos and statements about the vaccine will make your hair stand on end. Good luck finding some of them though. Most of his video interviews have been removed from social media. Here are just a few of his credentials:

- He co-discovered the AIDS virus with another physician.

- He won the coveted Nobel Prize in Medicine in 2008.

- He is a world-renowned virology expert.

- He has worked as a researcher at the Pasteur Institute in Paris and as a full-time professor at Shanghai Jiao Tong University in China.

This physician is a walking encyclopedia of virology information, not disinformation. You don't get the Nobel Prize for Medicine if you are a quack! He said some shocking things during interviews in April/May of 2020 regarding the origins of the coronavirus. This was well before the Wuhan lab-created virus was accepted as truth. This doctor called it before anyone else. When he appeared on France's CNews, he said COVID-19 was "not natural" and suggested this disease actually resulted from work done by molecular biologists. (Check out the video on France's CNews or YouTube. At the time of this writing, it is still there.) Here is what French virologist Luc Antoine Montagnier said during the interview:

We came to the conclusion that there was manipulation around this virus. To a part but I do not say the total . . . of the coronavirus of the bat, someone added sequences, in particular of HIV, the virus of AIDS . . . It is not natural. It's the work of professionals, of molecular biologists . . . A very meticulous work.

He was seen as a conspiracist at the time of the interview because no one was talking about the coronavirus being created in a lab. Remember back a couple years ago when everyone thought coronavirus came from an outside wet market on the dirty streets of Wuhan. Now even mainstream media is coming around to the fact this virus was molecularly engineered by humans from within the Wuhan lab. Anthony Fauci and gain of function studies weren't talked about then, but it sure is making headlines today. Fauci and Dr. Rand Paul have gone a few bloody rounds. Dr. Rand Paul is also a doctor who has boldly challenged the narrative of vaccines being forced on everyone. I wonder what will be uncovered next year, and the year after that?

U.S. Senator Ron Johnson held a medical symposium for the top doctors in the country on January 24, 2022. He invited doctors from BOTH sides of the debate. Democrat and Republican, right and left. In fact, the invitation went out to the CDC director, FDA director, and Mr. Science himself- Dr. Fauci. You can watch the physician's discussion on Rumble. (Search "Second Opinion" or "Senator Ron Johnson"). It was absolutely incredible to hear each of these physician's bios and clinical expertise. These doctors were the best of the best. All of them were highly qualified doctors with some lengthy titles and research behind their names. Sadly, Fauci and friends didn't show up. I wonder why? Below is the actual outline for the symposium:

COVID-19: A Second Opinion
Moderator

Senator Ron Johnson (R-Wis.)

Medical experts and doctors

Four Pillars of Pandemic Response

- **Dr. Peter McCullough**

Pillar 1: Limit the spread

- **Dr. Bret Weinstein**

- **Dr. Jay Bhattacharya**

Pillar 2: Early at Home Treatment

- **Dr. Ryan Cole**

- **Dr. Harvey Risch**

- **Dr. George Fareed**

- **Dr. Pierre Kory**

- **Dr. Richard Urso**

Pillar 3: Hospital Treatment

- **Dr. Paul Marik**

- **Dr. Aaron Kheriaty**

Pillar 4: Vaccines

- **Dr. Robert Malone**

- **Dr. David Wiseman**

WHAT: Panel discussion on the global pandemic response, what went right, what went wrong, what should be done now, and what needs to be addressed long term. The panel will also discuss censorship from Big Tech and the mainstream media, pandemic response effect on children, and vaccine mandate impact on worker shortage.

WHEN: Monday, Jan. 24

      9 a.m. – 12 p.m. ET

WHERE: Russell Senate Office Building, Kennedy Caucus Room

      325

In addition to doctors and academicians, the Senator has also extended an invitation to the following federal health agency heads, the CEO's of Pfizer and Moderna, and other individuals who have developed, promoted, and led the response to the pandemic over the last two years:

- **Dr. Rochelle P. Walensky**, MD, MPH, Director of the Centers for Disease Control and Prevention

- **Dr. Janet Woodcock**, MD, Acting Commissioner of the U.S. Food and Drug Administration

- **Dr. Anthony S. Fauci**, MD, Director of the National Institute of Allergy and Infectious Diseases and Chief Medical Advisor to the President

- **Dr. Lawrence A. Tabak**, DDS, Ph.D., Acting Director of the National Institutes of Health

- **Jeffrey D. Zients**, White House Coronavirus Response Coordinator

- **Dr. Albert Bourla**, DVM, Ph.D., Chairman and Chief Executive Officer of Pfizer

- **Dr. Ugur Sahin**, MD, Chief Executive Officer of BioNTech

- **Stéphane Bancel**, MBA, Chief Executive Officer of Moderna

Therapeutics

- **Dr. Ashish K. Jha**, MD, MPH, Dean of Brown University School of Public Health

- **Dr. John R. Raymond Sr.**, MD, President and CEO of Medical College of Wisconsin

- **Dr. Jonathan Reiner**, MD, Professor of Medicine and Director of Cardiac Catheterization Labs

- **Dr. Scott Gottlieb**, MD, Former Commissioner of the U.S. Food and Drug Administration

- **Dr. Francis S. Collins**, MD, Ph.D., Former Director of the National Institutes of Health

- **Dr. Rick Bright,** Ph.D., Former Director of Biomedical Advancement Research and Development Authority

Besides no one showing up from the other side of the debate, which is pretty telling in and of itself, I have some other questions: Why doesn't mainstream media have these world-renowned physicians on their nightly news? Why does YouTube, Twitter, and others ban this symposium so it has to be put on Rumble, GETTR, and other outlets? What are they afraid of? Why is information from the world's leading physicians and health care organizations not being talked about on major news outlets like CNN, NBC, and the like? Why isn't there a healthy medical debate surrounding the vaccines, side effects, and effective protocols to treat Covid? Historically, that has been the process of how the best medicine and public health policy is decided upon.

Furthermore, why aren't the CDC, FDA, or other government-run health agencies examining and replicating what states with the lowest Covid rates are doing? For example, Florida has the lowest Covid rate per capita in the United States. That's not a political slant; it's a well-known statistical fact. It is also a well-known fact Florida has the least number of mandates, both mask and vaccine, in the entire country. Why isn't that being discussed on mainstream media each evening? Don't we all want to have the lowest number of Covid cases in our state? Deep down, even if we are left-wing democrats from California, don't we all want to live free like they do down in Florida? I want to move down there right now!

Why isn't the trustworthy CDC putting those facts front and center in their communications to the public? Wouldn't it be a timely message for the health and safety of our entire country if we could replicate Florida's low Covid rates? Is it because Ron DeSantis and Florida don't fit into a certain narrative the government and Big Pharma are trying to push? Because it certainly is not about your health and the actual science. If it was, as a country, we would be implementing the exact Covid protocols nationwide that exist in states like Florida. Oh, and by the way, Florida's economy is one of the best in the country.

CHAPTER 5

Children: COVID-19 Vaccine

Our goal is to vaccinate every child who walks through our door.
—Pediatrician

The above quote came from a leading pediatrician in my territory after I asked him what his views on vaccinating children were. What is interesting about his statement is our conversation took place *before* the Covid vaccine was ever approved for children. This particular pediatrician practices at a very large pediatric group located within my territory. This pediatrician also sits on a local pediatric board that determines vaccination protocols for thousands upon thousands of children.

I want to share the exact conversation I had with this physician regarding Covid vaccines and children. The conversation took place during a lunch I had with this doctor after I was done detailing him. In the pharmaceutical industry, a "detail" is where you sell the doctor on the benefits of your drug. You detail the doctor about how your specific medication can benefit the doctor's patients. It is standard practice to bring lunch into an office to get time with the doctors in order to detail them. (I am one of those guys in a suit who walks right back to see the doctor while you have been waiting over an hour. When I am waiting to see my personal physician, these drug reps irritate me as well!)

Early on in the pandemic I made a professional decision never to bring up the topic of the Covid vaccines in my offices because it had become such a divisive issue. Plus, the debate wouldn't really help my sales numbers. But if a doctor brought it up, I would engage. So, this lunch was business as usual. We discussed how the product I sell could help his patients. It was a pretty standard lunch detail that I have done thousands of times in my career.

I was completely finished with my detail; all business discussion about my product helping his patients had taken place. I shared from our package insert (the FDA-approved verbiage about a medication) how my product can greatly help his patients suffering from a specific medical condition that my product is FDA approved for. I then shared the specifics of the managed care (insurance) coverage of our product. The medication I sell is on a wide variety of insurance plans, so his patients can get our medication at an affordable price. I then went over our savings/co-pay cards outlining how his patients can save on our medication. Lastly, I followed up by answering a specific question this provider had about the coverage of our medication related to a local insurance plan most of his patients are enrolled in. All in all, it was a successful detail.

After my detail this pediatrician and I got into some small talk about sports and other current events. (I love calling on pediatricians because they are some of the most laid-back and easiest doctors on the planet to talk to.) One of the current events he brought up was Covid and the vaccines. A hot topic every night on the news was whether or not the vaccine is safe for children. At this time, the vaccine was not yet approved for kids, and the CDC was in the process of making this critical decision. As a pediatrician, I am sure this was top of mind for him.

As he continued talking about Covid, I specifically asked him his opinion on vaccinating children with the new Covid vaccines. I wanted to know what a leading pediatrician's views and opinions were on this current hot topic. After all, I have kids myself. Keep in mind, this doctor had no idea what my views were on the vaccine, or even if I was vaccinated. I am very careful to keep my own opinions on the matter private when in my offices. But if a physician initiates, I will ask a few questions so I can learn about this complex and ever-changing pandemic. I have daily access to very well-educated people who have devoted their entire lives to the practice of medicine. And I can always learn a lot from my physicians, especially about such a perplexing topic as COVID-19 and the vaccines:

Me: I hear discussion on the news each night regarding Covid vaccines and children. As a pediatrician, what is your opinion on vaccinating children?

Doc: Our goal is to vaccinate every child who walks through our door. And I can't wait for it to be approved so I can vaccinate my own children.

Me: I read a recent statement the Cleveland Clinic made about the Covid vaccines, "Natural immunity is superior to vaccinated immunity." Some top physicians and researchers at the Cleveland Clinic claim natural immunity is actually better. What is your take on the Cleveland Clinic's statement about natural immunity versus vaccinated immunity? (This guy is a pediatrician in a very busy practice. I really wanted to know his thoughts on natural immunity.)

Doc: (He sort of brushed off my question, taking another bite of his dessert.) Not in this case, vaccinated immunity is better. (He said this without flinching, not even acknowledging the Cleveland Clinic is a pretty reputable organization.)

I was surprised this pediatrician made such a matter-of-fact claim that was not really backed up by well-known science. Every virologist in the world knows that natural immunity always trumps vaccinated immunity—especially in the case of viruses, because a virus will always mutate and make new and different strains of the original virus. When this happens, the body develops natural immunity to fight the new strains. Most virologists know that you simply can't make a vaccine to protect against every new strain. But maybe he knew something I didn't, so I asked another question:

Me: One of your colleagues I call on suggested I watch a video by Dr. Robert Malone. He is the doctor who developed mRNA technology, which the vaccines are founded upon. In this video Dr. Malone said the vaccines are "leaky" and "dangerous." He said they are leaky because they wear off in about six months. And he said they were dangerous because a slew of serious side effects is being reported to VAERS. What do you think of statements like this from one of the leading virologists in the world who developed mRNA technology?

Doc: That's just misinformation, and there is a lot of it out there.

That was it! No scientific explanation, no citing of opposing articles or research. With an air of superiority, he just told me the inventor of mRNA technology, who spent the last thirty years of his career devoted to developing safe and efficacious vaccines for society, Dr. Robert Malone, was spreading misinformation. I was shocked.

I didn't say anything further because I could tell he was doubled down on his stance and no amount of scientific data was going to change that. I ended the conversation by saying, "Interesting, good info to know, thanks for sharing." End of discussion. I thanked him for his time, and he went back to seeing his patients. I said goodbye to the other staff in the lunchroom, collected my belongings, and headed out to see my next office.

I walked out of his office flabbergasted at what I had just heard from a leading pediatrician in the area. He totally disregarded a legitimate study the Cleveland Clinic put out on the advantages of natural immunity over vaccinated immunity. And then he completely disregarded statements from the inventor of mRNA technology as "misinformation." I was flabbergasted. But this was his view, and he was entitled to it. I hopped in my car and drove off to see my next office.

However, I couldn't get that conversation out of my mind the rest of the day because it seemed this pediatrician was under some sort of Jedi mind control. He wasn't even willing to entertain scientific data that differed from his own viewpoint. I shared this story with my wife when I got home from work that evening. The conversation kept rolling around in my head as I tried to process the absurdity of a leading pediatrician in my territory ready and willing to vaccinate children before the vaccine was even approved for them. What was up with that? It didn't make any sense. There wasn't even any long-term safety data out yet regarding children and the vaccine. Most pharmaceuticals and vaccines take about five years to go through all the phases/trials to determine efficacy and safety. Just from a sheer legal standpoint alone, as a pediatrician, I would never be injecting children with an experimental vaccine.

This event let me know how lethal the narrative of this vaccine has become. For a pediatrician, who sits on the vaccination board in a major metropolitan area, to have the goal to vaccinate every child who walks through his door before the vaccine was ever approved for children is absolutely insidious. He shrugged off legitimate sources, like the Cleveland Clinic and the inventor of mRNA technology, as frivolous and misinformation. It didn't cross his mind for a moment that maybe he was the one misinformed.

I still can't figure out why doctors and health officials are ignoring such facts as the dismal VAERS data related to the vaccine, legitimate articles like those from the Cleveland Clinic, top virologists in the world like mRNA inventor Dr. Robert Malone, and one of the most respected cardiologists in the world, Dr. Peter McCullough. But then again, money talks, doesn't it? Take a look at Pfizer's earnings over the last six months. Their stock price is up +34.77% from July 2021 to January 2022. Of course, this narrative is recklessly propagated without a second thought. When major pharmaceutical companies and big executives stand to make a fortune, nothing can get in the way, not even truth.

I was absolutely horrified that this doctor in a large pediatric group was hell-bent on vaccinating every kid who came through their door before ever seeing any long-term safety data. The issue of side effects, like myocarditis that we are now seeing extensively in the younger population, was not even considered by this physician. What was going on here?

The sad truth is, many doctors are misinformed. This guy wasn't out to hurt children; he really believes in what he is doing. But he is treating children, and extra safety measures should be taken. Even pediatricians, those treating our most vulnerable of patients, are buying lock, stock, and barrel the narrative that vaccines are essential for children. Never mind the VAERS data shows over twenty thousand deaths associated with the vaccine and over one million adverse events reported such as blood clots and myocarditis.

The diabolical thing about all of this is many doctors are not really following the science. (Many, however, are, and we will get to that.) Many doctors out there are just taking verbatim what CNN and the White House are claiming as facts. Even when the science does not back up these so-called facts, the doctors won't back down. For instance, months on end we heard in mainstream media that the unvaccinated were to blame for the spread of Covid. Biden even said in one of his press conferences he was, "Getting impatient with the unvaccinated," and this was a, "pandemic of the unvaccinated." Even though the data was already out and perfectly clear that both unvaccinated and vaccinated spread the virus, the White House did not change their tune. And sadly, neither are some physicians.

I run into three types of physicians out in the field. The first type is those like this pediatrician. They just blindly follow what "science" is being pushed down from the top without really thinking for themselves. These physicians are badly misinformed. They aren't intentionally setting out to hurt their patients. They completely believe in what they are doing. But these doctors are playing Russian roulette with their patients' lives and health because they are believing in one of the most powerful false narratives ever perpetrated against the American public, and for that matter, the entire world.

A second type of physician is those who are just plain scared. Afraid to lose their jobs, they just go along with directives handed down to them by the large health care organizations they work for. One of my physician friends showed me a letter threatening her job if she prescribed ivermectin, a medicine she has seen help her patients recover from Covid and keep them out of the hospital. Your doctor is under a tremendous amount of pressure.

The other type of physician is those who stand their ground and give their patients the best care, regardless of the consequences. If a medication helps their patient and is safe, they write it. Even if they could get into trouble, they do what is right for their patient. This is the type of doctor you want. If you have a doctor who panders to political correctness and gives into the bullying of big corporations, you will not get the best care for yourself and your family. But in my experience, this is only about 30 percent of the physicians out there. And they are hard to find. Of all physician types, pediatricians should be the most concerned about the safety of the Covid vaccines. After all, they are treating our future generation.

CHAPTER 6

Systemic Vaxism

Oh, you're one of *those people*!
—Internal Medicine Doctor

The quote above was said to me by an internal medicine doctor I call on. It took place during a lunch detail at a large medical office in my territory. Very similarly to my lunch with the pediatrician, I detailed this internal medicine doctor about how my product can help her patients struggling with a specific disease. We had a robust conversation about how my medication can truly bring relief to her patients suffering from a debilitating condition. We covered the clinical benefits my medication would provide to even her hardest-to-treat patients. I also went over the great managed care coverage my product has. We talked extensively about the product, savings cards, etc. I covered it all. Other doctors were also in the lunchroom engaged in the discussion. It was a very productive sales call.

When we were clearly done with the business portion of our conversation, we engaged in some small talk. Then the doctor brought up the Covid vaccine. This lunch took place about a year or so into the pandemic, and like now, everyone was still trying to make sense of it all. Vaccine mandates didn't yet exist. Here is how the conversation went down:

Doc: My husband will probably have to get revaccinated because the vaccine efficacy wears off in about six months.

Me: Why does the efficacy wear off in six months?

Doc: They are not sure yet, but it has to do with the spike protein.

Me: What do you think of other treatment options out there like hydroxychloroquine?

Doctor: No, that doesn't work. We only do the vaccine. (I was surprised at this statement because she had just got done telling me the vaccines wear off in about six months and her husband would need another shot.)

Doctor: Are you vaccinated?

Me: No, not yet. I want to wait and see more safety data since the vaccines just came out.

Doctor: Oh, you're one of *those people*! (She said this in a very demeaning and insulting tone.)

End of conversation.

Now, I wanted to say so many things in response to that derogatory term: "those people." It was a vaxist jab against all the inferior and uneducated deplorables who just don't know any better. But it made no sense she was judging someone who was unvaccinated after she just shared that her husband's vaccine was waning.

I honestly wanted to chime back, "Oh yeah, by one of *those people* you mean someone who doesn't want to take an experimental drug that actually killed mice in early treatment protocols. Or one of those people who doesn't trust everything CNN or the government is telling us. (Looking back on it now, it doesn't seem like Chris Cuomo, former CNN anchor, was all that trustworthy anyway.) Or one of those people who actually listens to one of the top virologists in the world who calls the vaccines 'leaky' and 'dangerous.' Yeah, I'm one of *those people*."

But of course, I showed some self-restraint. I didn't want to belittle her like she just did me. Plus, I wanted to keep my job. So I just smiled while she went on a systemic vaxism tirade. She bustled about the lunchroom and ate her dessert, we engaged in some small chit-chat about the weather or whatever else was on her mind, and then she went back to seeing her patients.

The next time I was in that office, the office manager quietly ushered me over and under her breath whispered, "Are you vaccinated?" I leaned in and whispered back, "It's a violation of HIPAA to ask me about my personal medical records. You are whispering because you know you shouldn't be asking. Let's make a deal . . . You tell me what diseases and disorders you have, like AIDS, sexually transmitted diseases, herpes, anti-anxiety meds, diabetes meds, etc., and then I will tell you if I have been vaccinated." Now, I actually didn't say that, but I really wanted to. I simply said, "No, I am not vaccinated."

Clearly this doctor was upset with me because I was unvaccinated. She ran and told the office manager to question me the next time I was in. But this doctor was simply parroting the nightly narrative she heard on CNN. And it's no wonder. It is a powerful narrative being pushed every second of every day. The one-size-fits-all mantra demanding vaccines for everyone has most of the free world living in a police state of fear. And if you go against this narrative, you are just stupid, and furthermore you could be a domestic terrorist. In her mind, I was the scum of the earth because I was unvaccinated. Plus, I mentioned a therapeutic alternative Donald Trump himself took, even though I never mentioned politics or Donald Trump. (I never bring up politics in my offices. It is unprofessional and too divisive.) I find it extremely troubling that even doctors are not interested in following the science, but only a narrative being pushed by a very crooked mainstream media.

Because of her political leanings, not mine, I was framed as the devil for not getting vaccinated. Furthermore, how dare I mention a therapeutic alternative to the vaccine which helped Donald Trump recover from Covid. She figured I was a Republican, and since she is a Democrat, anything coming out of my mouth is misinformation. Never mind her husband's leaky vaccine experience. Her politics and hatefulness for anything conservative or Donald Trump made her classify me as "one of *those people*." Her politics trumped the science (pun intended).

It's kind of funny though. Well, not really funny, but truly sad. If I had said to this doctor, "Oh, you're one of *those people*," because she got an experimental drug that has had some serious side effects—one of them being death! I would have been immediately thrown out of this office, a call would have been made to my manager, and I would have been looked at like a "racist" against the vaccinated. But if she said it, that was totally fine. The double standard today is palpable.

I have told this story to other doctors and administrators who also work for this same large health care organization. They were appalled a doctor in their organization would make such a derogatory comment. It's sad, but this is where we are at as a society. There are "those people," the unvaccinated. And then there are the vaccinated. What happened to the promise of unity coming from the presidential pulpit? It has become so politicized. We can't even get to the truth of what is working and what is not. And if we can't get to the truth, we won't get to a solution.

Two of my very best friends are vaccinated. One sincerely regrets getting the vaccine, and the other doesn't understand why I wouldn't just get it. He even said to me, "Trump is the one who got the vaccines pushed through. Why wouldn't you get the vaccine since you voted for Trump?" I told him this wasn't politics for me. It's about the science—the real science and data I am seeing regarding the vaccine. The fact that millions of folks who voted for Trump have not gotten the jab should be evident this goes well beyond politics. It's about a vaccine that doesn't work and causes more harm than good in many cases. It's about the science—the real science behind the vaccine. Not the politics.

Speaking of Big Government and Big Pharma, a Pfizer scientist was recently caught on camera stating that natural immunity is better protection against COVID-19 than the vaccine. Go to Project Veritas if you want to check out a senior scientist from Pfizer actually admitting natural immunity is better than the Pfizer vaccine. The FBI has since raided the house of James O'Keefe, founder of Project Veritas, and labeled him a terrorist for putting out these real-life interviews with Pfizer employees. I guess there is a price to pay for being one of *those people*. Kind of reminds me of the FBI labeling Virginian parents "domestic terrorists" for challenging what the school system is teaching their children. We all know how that turned out. Virginia just flipped Republican because of gross government overreach.

CHAPTER 7

Ivermectin: What's the Big Deal?

I will get fired if I prescribe ivermectin.
—Multiple physicians

Thus far I have shared about physicians who are all-in on the draconian mandate of vaccinating everyone, including our children. These folks would be best friends with former NYC mayor, Bill de Blasio, if they had the chance. They are pro-boosters every six months, wearing two masks with a face shield, and showing your vaxport before going into a McDonald's. I am going to switch gears here and talk about the other side of the story: physicians who are dead set against the mandate, don't get the vaccine themselves, and encourage therapeutics instead of the vaccine to treat their patients. This is what you don't hear about in mainstream media. And if you watch mainstream media, these stories will come as a complete shock to you. But remember, these are real doctors treating real patients. And they have shared their stories with me.

So, what's the deal with ivermectin anyway? It has gained a lot of attention in the news as of late. There are certain things about ivermectin you need to know. Let's take a look at the science, doctors, and Big Pharma as it relates to this supposed horse dewormer.

What actually is ivermectin? Well, for starters, ivermectin won the Noble Prize for Medicine in 2015—for humans! Let me say again: ivermectin has helped so many people, with so few side effects, that doctors all over the world voted this drug to win the Noble Prize for Medicine. Not a bad thing to have on your resume if you are a drug. It is also on the WHO (World Health Organizations) list of essential medicines. To be clear, these ivermectin accolades were for treatment in HUMANS, not horses. (Look on Wikipedia if you want confirmation.) Yes, it can also be used for horses. But ivermectin become an award-winning drug for its antiviral treatment in humans.

If you watch mainstream media, they paint ivermectin as this horse dewormer which can kill you on the spot if you take it. What is even worse, the FDA has put out false adds and statements about ivermectin. One such add states, "You are not a horse. You are not a cow. Seriously, y'all. Stop it…Using ivermectin to treat COVID-19 can be dangerous and even lethal. The FDA has not approved the drug for that purpose." Shame on the FDA! It is diabolical to call ivermectin dangerous when their own statistics from VAERS show otherwise. Let's survey the FDA and CDC's data on ivermectin.

VAERS data from 1996 – 2021. Deaths per year for each of the following medications:

- **Ivermectin**   **15**

- Hydroxychloroquine   69

- Tylenol   1,024

- Remdesivir   921
  (Since 2020)

- **COVID-19 Vaccines   20,175**
  (13 months)

How dare the FDA use fear tactics and false claims about any drug. Especially a drug that won the Nobel Prize for Medicine and is on the WHO's essential list of medicines. The FDA's own data shows ivermectin is one of the safest and most effective drugs of all time. When the FDA is putting out false claims and fear mongering the American people regarding a medicine shown to be safe by their **own** data over the last twenty-six years, we have more than a problem, we have obscene corruption at the highest level.

I watched CNN one evening and they literally kept calling ivermectin a horse dewormer without ever mentioning it is one of the most widely used medicines in humans of all time. And of course, they didn't mention it won the Noble Prize for Medicine in 2015—for humans. This was not journalism; it was simply misinformation. The fact CNN shouted from the rooftops that ivermectin was only indicated for use in horses was awfully misleading, the journalist reporting the misinformation should have been fired on the spot. Oh wait, Chris Cuomo was fired, but not for that. And just recently two CNN producers resigned for soliciting sex with minors. Nice clean organization over there . . . very trustworthy.

Hold on to your seats. Here is where the ivermectin story gets even more interesting. As previously shared, many of the physicians I call on are very close friends. They share a lot of information with me they wouldn't dare share with a rep who has only been calling on them for a couple of years. A number of these physicians have told me to come into their office and close the door. Although ivermectin has been helping their patients recover from Covid, they are being told from the top down to stop prescribing ivermectin or they will be fired. I was at my buddy's house one evening who is also a physician I call on. He showed me the threatening email he received from his large health care organization stating that if he prescribed ivermectin he would be investigated and possibly terminated.

Wrap your head around this for a second. Although ivermectin is actually helping patients recover, and recover quicker from Covid, physicians are being threatened with their jobs if they prescribe it. What's behind this rationale? Is it patient care? Is it treating patients with the best drug available? What's really going on here?

Pfizer just came out with their new version of ivermectin. It's called Paxlovid. On December 22, 2021, the FDA approved this new antiviral drug to treat Covid. Now why would they come out with a biosimilar drug to ivermectin if doctors aren't currently allowed to prescribe ivermectin? After all, ivermectin is readily available and cheap. Well, there you have it. Ivermectin is generic. And you guessed it, in Big Pharma, that means there is no money in it. But they can sure make a ton of money on Paxlovid. (Which really should be called Pfizermectin). It will be on patent and cost a whole heck of a lot more than generic ivermectin. I guarantee you physicians won't be fired for writing this "new" wonder drug. Instead, they will be encouraged and compensated to prescribe it. This is absolutely sinister! And it's happening at a local doctor's office near you.

My personal physician believes in ivermectin and other therapeutics like hydroxychloroquine which have proven efficacy to keep patients out of the hospital and recover quicker from Covid. He wrote me a prescription for ivermectin so I could have it on hand if I get Covid. I will never forget what happened when I called Walgreens to make sure my prescription was ready for pick up. Here's the conversation I had with the pharmacy tech:

Me: Yes, I am calling to make sure my prescription for ivermectin is ready before I come to pick it up.

Pharmacy tech: Yes, it's ready. But why did your doctor write you such a large quantity of ivermectin?

Me: What do you mean, such a large quantity? (I was intrigued about how this conversation would go.)

Pharmacy tech: The pharmacist doesn't recommend taking that high of a dose.

Me: Well, what dose does the pharmacist recommend? Is the pharmacist there? Let me talk to him or her.

Pharmacy tech: Hold on, let me get her . . . Oh, sorry, she said she can't advise you on what quantity to take since she is not your doctor. And by the way, ivermectin is used on horses as a dewormer.

Me: That's right, she's not my doctor. And actually, ivermectin won the Noble Prize for Medicine in 2015 . . . FOR HUMANS! Fill my script.

I went through a major bout of anxiety and depression five years ago because I had a bad accident and couldn't exercise for almost a year. Not moving was not good for me. I'm one of those guys who do triathlons just for fun. During my recovery, my physician prescribed me some pretty hard-core pharmaceuticals to get me through a very dark period in my life. He prescribed Ambien to help me sleep, a benzo to help with my anxiety, and a few other meds that are very addictive, habit forming, and had some pretty gnarly side effects. When I called this same Walgreens to get my prescriptions filled for these medications, the pharmacy tech never once asked me why I was taking these very habit-forming drugs. These drugs had a horrible safety profile when compared to ivermectin. Yet, when I called to get ivermectin, you would have thought I was picking up a kilo of cocaine.

I shared this story with my physician, and he was livid, as he should have been. A 24-year-old pharmacy tech was questioning my doctor's recommendations. He has known me for 17 years; Walgreen's doesn't know me except for my copay. What a gross overreach of a pharmacy tech questioning an MD who has over twenty-five years of experience.

There is something deeply disturbing about what's going on with this vaccine and the mandate. Doctors being forbidden to prescribe such drugs as ivermectin is a huge red flag. And at the same time *Pfizermectin* is currently out on the market. What's up with that? In seventeen years as a drug rep, I have never heard of doctors being threatened with their job for prescribing a drug that's helping their patients. Fortunately, there are bold and brave doctors out there who are defying these ludicrous orders.

One doctor friend of mine told me she still writes ivermectin, but she has to lie about the diagnosis to get it to go through. "Whatever it takes to help my patients," she told me. Now that's a great doc! However, many doctors are misinformed. And even those who know the real deal are running scared. They have families to provide for and mouths to feed. So, understandably, many doctors simply cave and don't write the best drug for their patients. I don't agree with that approach, but I certainly can understand it.

Communication from the CDC, WHO, and other government run medical agencies are ultimately responsible for pushing this diabolical dogma. Eventually these ridiculous polices makes it to the twenty-four-year-old pharmacy tech, who is just following orders. But what's even more concerning is these new regulations are also being implemented by the large HCO's your doctor works for. And now, doctors are even following these guidelines. Some doctors still trust the CDC, FDA, and other government-run agencies that were once trustworthy. But times have changed. If your physician is robotically following mandates being handed down to them, ultimately from huge corporate or government agencies with profit as their guiding principle, then you and your family will not get the best care from your doctor.

This brings up something else. Agencies like the CDC, FDA, and WHO used to be trustworthy. It's hard not to trust agencies that used to be truly patient-centric. However, the goalposts have moved. These entities are no longer worthy of taking at face value what they say. Sadly, they can't be trusted anymore. They are in bed with Big Pharma, Big government, and other outside forces who don't have your best interest in mind.

On a side note, many of the best physicians I call on grew up in communist countries like Poland and Russia. These physicians often tell me to come inside their office and close the door. What they tell me behind closed doors, in expletives, is amazing to hear. They say what's going on in America feels eerily similar to growing up in a communist country. They experienced the same sort of repression firsthand as a kid, so they would know. Lack of free speech, government control/gross overreach, and even a personal story of an uncle taken away to prison never to be seen again because he openly criticized the government. Maybe he was first labeled a domestic terrorist for simply questioning what the school system was teaching his children? Then he got taken away. We better wake the hell up!

Speaking of the CDC, a very interesting turn of events recently took place regarding the Johnson & Johnson vaccine. The situation is eerily similar to what the CDC has done to ivermectin, which is essentially giving it bad press and banning it to consumers. On December 16, 2021 the CDC recommended Americans choose to receive one of two other authorized COVID-19 vaccines over the Johnson & Johnson COVID-19 vaccine. The CDC's move came after its Advisory Committee on Immunization voted unanimously to make the recommendation in favor of the mRNA vaccines made by Moderna and Pfizer/BioNTech over the J&J shot.

Now, let's be perfectly clear here: the J&J vaccine is just as "authorized" as Pfizer and Moderna. I actually believe it's safer because J&J's vaccine uses a technology based on a modified version of an adenovirus to spur immunity in recipients, while the other two authorized vaccines use messenger RNA technology. In plain English: J&J is more like an old-school, traditional vaccine. The other two have a newer technology *not* tried and true on humans. But I digress. A drug is either safe or it's not. It's either on the market or pulled from the market.

It is absolutely ludicrous the CDC is recommending one drug over the other. The FDA and CDC's job is **not** to recommend one drug over another. They can pull a drug for being unsafe, not promote one drug over the other. That's the job of your doctor when discussing the best medication for your malady. This is absolutely diabolical! The real deal is Pfizer and Moderna, through lobbyists, have paid the government a lot more money than J&J. On a side note: In 2016, Big Pharma spent $246 million on lobbyists. This was more than was spent by defense and corporate lobbyists combined. This is all about money, not your safety. Pfizer and Moderna have just as many blood clots and adverse events as J&J, probably even more.

J&J just hasn't paid the big money to the extent Pfizer and Moderna have. There are so many more side effects to the mRNA vaccines that the CDC, FDA, and government don't want us to know about. Why else would there be a law now in place stating the general public can't see the data related to Covid vaccine safety and efficacy for another fifty years? Yeah, there really is a law making COVID-19 vaccine data a secret for the next fifty years! Thank God some folks in congress are pushing back against this insanity!

Ivermectin's not only been banned from being written by physicians, it's also not available anymore at big pharmacies like CVS and Walgreen's. Remember, whatever works to truly treat Covid cuts into Big Pharma and Big Government's goals of money and power. Ivermectin is not banned because it's unsafe. It is one of the most prescribed and safest drugs of all time. That's why it won the Noble Prize for Medicine. It's banned because it goes directly against the false narrative that everyone needs to take the vaccine. It's really this simple: less ivermectin = more vaccines, and more vaccines = more profit. When was the last time your physician got a letter threatening his or her job because they prescribed a drug that won the Noble Prize for Medicine and is helping their patients? We are living in perilous times.

CHAPTER 8

Adverse Events

> After my second Pfizer dose, I broke out in shingles and had a
> rash all over my face. I had to take a nap every day for four to five
> months because I was completely exhausted.
>
> **—A Close Friend**

The above quote is an adverse event a very close friend of mine experienced after receiving the second dose of the Pfizer vaccine. Friends and family have also told me numerous other adverse events they have experienced. And to be fair, other friends and family have gotten the vaccine and seem to be just fine so far.

Doctors, nurses, and hospital administrators on the frontline have also told me accounts of severe adverse events from the vaccine. I believe this is just one significant reason why many frontline healthcare workers have chosen NOT to get vaccinated, thus, the large turnouts of healthcare workers protesting the vaccine mandate all across our great country. You don't risk your job if something is truly safe and effective.

Thousands of health care workers are defying the mandate, protesting, and getting fired from their jobs. A good question to ask yourself is, why? Why would all of these healthcare workers be willing to risk their livelihoods if the vaccines were truly working the way they should? After all, they see firsthand day in and day out what happens to patients who get the vaccine. What are they truly seeing? This is a most important question to consider.

A bigwig in our company told me this when he went to get the vaccine: "My physician had me take aspirin a week before and two weeks after getting the vaccine. He also had me exercise strenuously before, during, and after I received my vaccine to reduce the risk of blood clotting." Now, why in the heck are we blindly taking a vaccine where we have to take preventative measures so we don't have blood clots and possible death as a side effect! This is absolutely preposterous.

Below I am going to give a list of what doctors, hospital administrators, and nurses have told me has happened to some of their patients after receiving the vaccine. The doctors who have shared this with me have no skin in the game except patient care. They are very trustworthy folks who I have known for many years, and I would trust them with the care of my own family members. I will also share side effects that a few family members and friends experienced after receiving the vaccine.

To be clear and give fair balance, not everyone experiences negative side effects from the vaccine. It's only been a year, and time will tell. But as of now, there are plenty of people who have gotten the vaccine and appear to be fine. And, as previously stated, there are plenty of doctors in my territory who are totally for the vaccine and believe in it with all their heart. But we hear that narrative every day when we turn on the nightly news. That's why I am focused on the other side of the story. We repetitively hear that everyone should not only be vaccinated, but also now receive the booster for ultimate protection against Covid. (Remember, the vaccines are "leaky," that's why you need a booster every six months.) And now the mainstream mantra is to vaccinate children ages five to eleven. Infants six months old are now even being considered for Covid vaccination! If you know anything about vaccines, children, and immunity, then you know this is one of the most diabolical health care agendas ever perpetrated on the general public. It's one thing to vaccinate the elderly or those with severe comorbidities, but it's quite another to vaccinate children. Every virologist, at least ones with half a brain, know kids have great immune systems and vaccination is a last resort for children.

Think of the list below as insider trader information in the medical sense. In terms of your health, the Covid vaccines have been the most overhyped medical "stock" in the history of mankind. However, the real value of this stock is starting to be realized.

I will start with an email my wife got two nights ago from one of the women in her Bible Study group. This lady just got the booster. The email is actually from this woman's daughter, because the woman wasn't able to send an email after getting the booster shot:

> Hi, my mom has suddenly become almost disabled. The only thing different she has done is have the Covid booster. She has no use of her right arm and can't do any normal things herself like using the bathroom, dressing, bathing, even getting her own food or driving. She is in such extreme pain she can't sleep in the room alone because she wakes up with shooting pain worse than labor. She would know, as she has four kids. She has lost so much weight and is emotionally distraught over not knowing what is wrong and feeling like a burden to others. Your help and prayers are greatly appreciated. Thank you!

This is not some distant woman on a news story. It is a real mother of four who my wife actually knows. These are real incidences, in real people. Does everyone have negative side effects from the vaccines? No. But some do, and that's what's not being reported on your nightly news. That is what's so diabolical. Here's more:

» Many doctors are reporting their patients who got vaccinated still get Covid. And these cases are not just mild. Some are serious and wind up in the hospital even *after* getting vaccinated.

» Male, mid-seventies, stroke after first shot.

» Doctor friend reported to me: "One of my patients is still in the hospital due to a blood clot after getting vaccinated."

» Male (firefighter), mid-forties: "I have not felt the same since getting the vaccine five months ago." General malaise and brain fog.

» Doctor friend of mine: "I now have swollen lymph nodes after receiving the first shot. I'm not going to get the second shot."

» Nurse in one of my offices: "I broke out with a rash and red-bumps all over my body. Something's not right with this vaccine."

» Female, late forties, EXTREME fatigue and "brain fog" for four weeks. ZERO energy. She is highly intelligent (chemical engineer) and a super energetic person, never sick. The vaccine stressed her immune system to the point of exhaustion.

» Female, mid-sixties, lost her ability to walk with serious leg complications.

» Male, mid-thirties, had trouble moving his arms after getting the jab.

» Female, early fifties, blood pressure dropped dangerously low after receiving the vaccine. She literally had a morbid grey coloring to her face and skin.

There are many more negative side effects from the vaccines. Doctors, nurses, and staff tell me about them frequently. The majority of nurses and staff in one of the larger offices I call on will not get the vaccine. The office manager told me the reason her staff will not get the jab is because of the extensive side effects they have witnessed in their patients.

There are two specific patient side effects I want to highlight in more detail. The first is a seventy-year-old male who was in tremendous physical shape. He worked out almost every day, and in the words of the office manager overseeing his case, "He looked like a fifty-year-old. You wouldn't guess this gentleman was close to seventy. He is a workout fanatic and was strong as an ox. Within a week after getting the vaccine injected into his body, he was in the hospital with a number of serious side effects. He had a blood clot, his blood pressure was affected; instead of being tone and strong, his skin is now drooping under his arms because of rapid muscle loss. And he is hanging on to life by a thread."

This was all reported to me by a trusted friend who oversees the doctors and nurses in a large thriving multi-doctor practice in a very affluent part of town. Again, does this happen to everyone who gets the jab? No. But does it happen to some people? Yes. And not just a few outliers. The vaccines definitely impact enough patients negatively that many nurses and staff fear getting the jab. I would love to see mainstream media interview some of these folks on the frontline. But that would completely destroy their narrative.

The other incident I want to tell you about is a detailed conversation with a physician regarding cancer and the Covid vaccine. She has a thriving practice in a beautiful suburb where everyone wants to live. Schools are great, the real estate market is booming, and this physician has to turn a lot of potential patients away because she is so well respected. She primarily sees women in her practice.

I have a good relationship with this doctor and her staff, but I wouldn't consider her a close friend like some of my other physicians. She has no idea of my opinions or views on the vaccine, because I never initiate this conversion with my physicians. We were standing in the hallway, and she brought up Covid and the vaccines. I asked her what she thought about the vaccines. She shook her head back and forth sheepishly then whispered, "I don't really think the vaccines work, and furthermore, I definitely don't agree with the mandate." She wasn't bold with her statements. Instead, she was testing the waters with me since she had no idea of my Covid views. She then asked me what I thought, and I told her I agreed with her. Once she knew where I stood and wasn't some sort of vaccine police, she told me to come into her office and shut the door. She didn't want her patients to hear what she was about to share.

Once she closed her office door, she wasn't shy! She got going on quite a tirade of data she has seen that makes her sincerely question the validity and safety of the vaccines. She even suggested some of the data is linking Covid vaccines to a higher rate of breast cancer in women. She didn't say Covid caused breast cancer, but she affirmed it can definitely awaken the sleeping giant of breast cancer if a woman is so predisposed.

I had never heard this before and was shocked at this possibility. I then shared about a very close friend of ours who just got diagnosed with breast cancer. She asked me some questions about her. Our friend had no previous history of breast cancer in her entire family, not in her mother, grandmother, aunts, or sister. The only thing different she did regarding her health over the last few years was get the vaccine. The physician then told me she wouldn't be surprised at all if the vaccine activated an autoimmune response in this woman that essentially "turned on her cancer cells." I couldn't believe what I was hearing. She could see the unbelief and skepticism on my face, so she persisted.

This physician went on to tell me that any woman who gets vaccinated must wait six weeks before they can get a mammogram. She informed me this is common procedure and is written in all of the testing protocols for women getting a mammogram. She explained the reason for waiting is the vaccine causes the swelling of lymph nodes following the injection. Women must wait for the swelling and autoimmune response to calm down before getting a mammogram. That in and of itself was kind of scary. What if in some women the autoimmune response doesn't calm down? I went home that night and did some fact-checking of my own. Yep, she was right. This was standard procedure and common practice in all the articles I read related to women, mammograms, and the Covid vaccines.

I have never heard Fauci or mainstream media share this fact openly. Why is this not discussed at length on women's talk shows? Why doesn't Fauci or Biden address vaccine safety issues and serious side effects when addressing the nation? I have never heard the negative side of the Covid vaccines mentioned even once! Why not give a list of all the possible adverse events like you see on commercials for *every* pharmaceutical that has ever been marketed to the general public? It's actually required by the FDA for pharmaceutical companies to list out all the possible side effects when marketing a new medication. Why not do this for the vaccine as well? Here's the question: WHY ISN'T THE FDA MAKING PFIZER AND MODERNA LIST ALL OF THE NEGATIVE SIDE EFFECTS of the Covid vaccines? After all, the FDA has required this for every single drug that's ever been marketed?

All I have seen are PSAs (public service announcements) reminding us to stay safe and get the vaccine. No list of adverse events for this vaccine is being required. I have even seen public service announcements where little Timmy says, "All I want for Christmas is the vaccine." What ten-year-old kid would ever ask for a shot for Christmas? The kicker for me is *Sesame Street*'s public service announcement coercing and manipulating kids to get the vaccine. Big Bird's grandmother discusses why she chose to have Big Bird vaccinated. "I made the decision to get Big Bird vaccinated because COVID vaccines are the best way to keep yourself, our friends and neighbors, and me safe and healthy," Granny Bird then says in the PSA. "The vaccine is going to help my bird and all the kids out there stay safe and healthy." (Check it out, it's online.)

What's next, a PSA advocating kids take their Adderall so they can focus and get better grades? I can see Big Granny Bird saying, "Now, if you want to get A's like all the other good boys and girls, remember to take your Adderall." Have we completely lost our minds! I have never before seen any PSA marketing any pharmaceutical, especially not one to children. That's not the role of the government or *Sesame Street*.

What if the CDC, FDA, and other government-run health care agencies came out with an honest and true commercial about the vaccines in which they listed all of the negative side effects? You've seen those adds for the latest pharmaceutical where at the end of the commercial the narrator speeds up his or her cadence and says, "May cause blood clotting, liver damage, severe rash, bleeding from every orifice of your body, and even death." You still may want to take that pharmaceutical because, for you, the benefits outweigh the risks. And there is nothing wrong with that type of marketing. It gives fair balance to the benefits of the drug versus the risks. We can all live with that.

If the government health agencies put out ads like that related to the Covid vaccine, then maybe there wouldn't be such confusion. Then we could make up our own minds if the benefits outweigh the risks. Instead, we are mandated to take a drug that could cause serious harm or even death. And if we don't comply, we will get fired and be labeled domestic dissenters.

What if the entire world was mandated to take an ADHD medication? Clinical studies show they can help your focus, energy, mood, and even help you lose weight. Don't we all want that? Don't we all need that? What if Big Bird was telling every kid they needed to take their ADHD medicine to help them be better kids and create a better society? That sounds pretty good, right?

But, at the same time, what if they were not honest and forthcoming about the side effects? What if they didn't tell you from the clinical studies that the FDA has determined ADHD medicine can stunt the growth of children. It's a much tougher sell if Granny Big Bird says, "Johnny Bird will be better behaved and able to focus. But instead of being 6'3, he's only going to be 5'9." What if they didn't tell you the clinical studies of ADHD medicine showed they can cause a serious rise in your blood pressure? And what if they didn't tell you heart complications can result from taking these medications long term?

It still may be worth it for you to take your ADHD medicine. But now you truly know the inherent risks. You and your physician can determine if the desired benefits outweigh the possible risks.

The fact that we are not getting honest communication about the side effects of the Covid vaccine is absolutely diabolical. If any pharmaceutical company marketed a drug like this, there would be extensive lawsuits. And if a government also perpetrated this lie, they would also be held accountable. Guess what the next ten years are going to look like? That's right, major lawsuits against Big Pharma, Big Corporations, and Big Government. It's already begun.

CHAPTER 9

VAERS: Vaccine Adverse Event Reporting System

COVID-19 vaccines account for 3X more deaths than ALL other vaccines combined over the last 30 years.

—VAERS Data

In the last chapter we talked about adverse events that I have witnessed first-hand from doctors in the field, friends, and family. In this chapter we will delve further into VAERS, which is co-managed by both the FDA and CDC. Let's take a look at the most recent numbers related to the COVID vaccines and just a few of the adverse events.

COVID-19 Vaccine data through January 7, 2022:

21,745 – Deaths

25,773 – Myocarditis/Pericarditis

37,973 – Permanently Disabled

3,594 – Miscarriages

A Harvard study estimates less than 1% of all adverse events are actually reported to VAERS. Not every doctor, patient, and especially hospital organization reports every Covid related death or adverse event to VAERS. There are a couple reasons for this. One is the fear of losing funding if you go against the powerful narrative that the vaccines are safe and effective and should be taken by all. Large HCOs and big corporations are getting government funding, aka a boatload of money, for getting vaccination rates above 90% for their employees.

Another reason not every adverse event is reported is simply because it's a pain in the ass. It takes time and diligence to stop your extremely busy day as a doctor or hospital administrator to go into VAERS and actually do the tedious and time-consuming work of documenting an adverse event. And since adverse events do not directly benefit large hospital organizations or doctor groups, you can bet your bottom dollar a lot of adverse events, including death, get swept under the rug. Money talks; adverse events don't.

Let's talk a minute about one of the managing partners of VAERS, the CDC. The tag line for the CDC is, "24/7: Saving Lives. Protecting People." Sounds good to me. That's a pretty lofty goal. I like organizations that aim high. Here's the real deal on the CDC. This organization is more of a private nonprofit business than it is a government agency.

There is an entity called the CDC **Foundation**. This foundation operates under the auspice of the CDC. Nothing insidious so far. But let's take a closer look, "**The CDC** Foundation, which began operating in 1995, supports numerous program activities that extend the impact of **CDC**'s work. Although **the CDC** Foundation was chartered by Congress, it is **not** a **government** agency nor is it a division of **CDC**. It is a **private**, nonprofit organization . . ." (CDC website). Here's where it gets tricky. The CDC accepts private funding, not only government funding. You can see where there is a huge conflict of interest say if Pfizer or other pharmaceutical agencies fund the CDC

Foundation, which they do!

If a new pharmaceutical on the market has a certain number of serious adverse events reported, it is often pulled from the market because it is deemed unsafe for the general public. And if it had a few thousand deaths listed as one of the adverse events, then it would most certainly be pulled from the market. Let me put it this way: the vaccine safety data from the trials alone would have prevented the Covid vaccines from ever coming to market. Most of the animals that mRNA technology was trialed on either died or had very serious side effects. That is why it wasn't brought to market twenty years ago when it was tested on SARS.

I have sold pharmaceuticals that have black box warnings on their label. A black box warning is the gravest warning listed on a pharmaceutical since very serious adverse events like blood clots, myocarditis, and even death can occur as a result of taking the drug. These very same side effects that require a black box warning are commonplace among the Covid vaccines. Yet not even one black box warning? Why, why not even one warning saying, "Death has occurred in some individuals that have taken the vaccine as well as blood clots, myocarditis, irregular autoimmune response, shingles, severe rash and swelling, etc., etc.?" I don't have to tell you why; you are smart. Or just look at the stock price surge of Pfizer and Moderna over the last year, and it's pretty easy to figure out.

The government is in bed with Big Pharma. And mainstream media is the blanket covering them both, keeping them warm and cozy. Kickbacks galore are happening between the government, Big Pharma, and mainstream media. And this is nothing new. It's just now we are in the worst health pandemic of our lives. People are vulnerable and scared. So, to take advantage of people at such a time as this is absolutely reprehensible.

If you argue against this COVID narrative mandating every person take the vaccine, you are arguing against some tremendously powerful entities like Big Pharma, Big Government, and Big Tech. This unholy trinity wields enormous power and persuasion. Never mind what Dr. Robert Malone, Dr. Peter McCullough, and a number of other highly informed physicians say about the dangers of the vaccine and the power of natural immunity. If you question this one narrative, you are a rabid Trump supporter, probably a white supremacist, or just plain dumb. You know, one of *those people*.

Mainstream media, Biden's press conferences, and especially the pharmaceutical companies are extremely hush-hush about side effects and deaths that have occurred due to the COVID-19 vaccines. Makes you wonder if they really have our best interest in mind? I'm scared to see both the short-term and long-term effects of the vaccine. It's worth stating again: there is now an actual law preventing the full disclosure of safety data regarding the Covid vaccines for fifty years! It's a good thing that some folks in Congress are countering this law with another bill proposing full disclosure now.

Let me tell you how stringent pharmaceutical companies, the CDC, and the FDA usually are about the safety of a new drug that has just come out. I have launched and sold numerous pharmaceuticals during my career as a pharmaceutical representative. I want to tell you about one drug I sold that actually had its name completely changed after it was out on the market.

This drug had a very, very successful launch. The medication showed clinically significant efficacy and superb safety data during the five-year trial phase of the drug. (By the way, it usually takes about five years to get through all of the phases of a drug trial before a drug comes to the marketplace, not just a few months like the vaccines.) This particular drug had thousands of new-patient starts and favorable managed care coverage. Now, after a year on the market and a very successful launch, this drug had to get its name changed. And here is why.

Four patients nationwide received the wrong medication because the pharmacy tech gave them another drug similar in name. You see, the drug we launched was very close in name and pronunciation to another drug already on the market. That's why the pharmacy technicians made these errors. Again, let me stress, this was a total of only four patients nationwide. Now, this is a big deal because the safety of these four patients was compromised. Taking the wrong medication could kill you. Our company absolutely did the right thing. They should have changed the name, and I commend them for doing it. I am proud of the patient-centric approach my company practices.

This change cost our company millions of dollars in new marketing materials, branding, and samples. And we did it for the safety of only four individuals. What a cool company, right? Yes, very cool. It's refreshing when you see a big company, especially Big Pharma, do the right thing. **However**, now this very same Big Pharma company is making every employee get an experimental vaccine injected into their body that is proven to have serious side effects. And make no mistake about it, even though it's FDA approved, it is still very much in the experimental phase until the five-year safety data is released. It's too bad our company doesn't treat its thousands of employees as well as it did those four patients who got the wrong medication at the pharmacy. People in our company have been ruthlessly fired for not getting the vaccine.

If this vaccine was a new drug our company was launching, it would have never made it to market. And if it somehow did make it to the marketplace, it would have been pulled in the first two months because of far too many adverse reactions. You never would have heard about these vaccines ever again. But instead of doing the right thing like pulling the vaccines from the market or disclosing to the public the well-documented adverse events and deaths resulting from the vaccine, the negative side effects are being suppressed and hidden. Meanwhile, the safety and effectiveness of the vaccines continue to be the ruse of Big Pharma, mainstream media, and the government. Instead of saying, "Let's hold on a minute," they are now shouting, "Boosters for everyone!" The extent of vaccination gaslighting is astounding. We truly have been VAXLIT the last two years.

You used to be able to trust the big three news networks of ABC, CBS, and NBC. (And a while back CNN.) You also used to be able to trust government agencies like the FDA and CDC. The goalposts have changed. "We are not in Kansas anymore, Toto." Mainstream media and government health agencies are NOT separate entities from the government. They have now all become different branches of the Democratic party spewing out the same narrative with no critical thought.

Medicine has a rich history of tough debate and critical thinking behind it. It is all part of the scientific method to arrive at truth. However, critical debate surrounding the vaccine and questioning Fauci Almighty is seen as a pseudo terrorist act. Again, if you don't believe me, take a look at the parents in Virginia who were labeled domestic terrorists by the DOJ and FBI for questioning the school system about what it was teaching their children. The same rabid approach is being done to those questioning the legitimacy of the Covid vaccines.

We have gone so far off the rails as a country. Truth and the democratic process are being repressed at every turn. Kind of reminds you of communist countries in the past that suppress the truth and lock their people up if they don't comply. Wait, that's happening right now. Just look at countries like Australia and Germany who have nonvaccinated concentration camps where they are shuttling the unvaccinated to. That's not in the past; it's in the present. And if we don't wake up, America is next. One of my doctor friends who grew up in a communist country recently said to me, "I came to America to get away from this kind of tyranny. Now where do I go? This is absolutely %#$*&%#@! Ridiculous."

CHAPTER 10

Let's Go Brandon!

You can hear the chants from the crowd, "Let's Go Brandon!"
—NBC Sports Reporter Kelli Stavast

On October 2, Brandon Brown, NASCAR driver, won his first-ever NASCAR race. It was a big moment for him. When being interviewed by Kelli Stavast, NBC sports reporter, immediately following his victory, you could hear fans clearly chanting in the background, "F… Joe Biden." I couldn't believe my ears when I heard this reporter literally lying to millions of people who just watched this major NASCAR event. (If you are into tennis, this event is equivalent to winning a Grand Slam like Wimbledon. If you are into golf, this is equivalent to winning a major like The Masters.) The fans were clearly chanting, "F… Joe Biden." Yet this reporter basically told millions of folks watching this major NASCAR event they weren't hearing what they actually were hearing or seeing what they were actually seeing. Ricky Bobby wouldn't have put up with that shit. (Watch *Talladega Nights: The Ballad of Ricky Bobby* for context.)

The phrase, "Let's Go Brandon," caught on so quickly because people are fed up with the overreach of the Biden regime, for sure. But it's much more than that. It also caught on like wildfire because mainstream media was caught red-handed gaslighting the American people. In essence, mainstream media, which is just a puppet of the Democratic party, has been telling us we haven't been seeing what we are seeing or hearing what we are hearing. Kelli Stavast, the NASCAR reporter, captured the absurdity of mainstream media perfectly when she told the audience they were hearing one thing, while clearly what was being chanted was something entirely different. The entire American public has been gaslit like never before. Half of the country is ticked off, and the other half doesn't even know they've been lied to. This same dichotomy is taking place in countries all over the world.

The Wikipedia definition of *gaslighting*: "Gaslighting is a colloquialism that is loosely defined as 'making someone question their own reality'…The term may also be used to describe a person (*gaslighter*) who effectively puts forth a false narrative that leads another person or a group of people to doubt their own perceptions . . ." A false narrative is exactly what has been put forth to the American public, and for that matter, the entire world. If you listen long enough to mainstream democratic ideology, you start to question the reality happening all around you. Consider the slew of gaslighting the Biden administration has put forth this past year by mainstream media:

1. "The vaccines are safe and effective. EVERYONE, including children, should get vaccinated:" Anyone who questions this is causing the pandemic to get worse and in Joe Biden's own words, "This is a pandemic of the unvaccinated." Now we know unvaccinated **and** vaccinated alike can transmit the disease. Even CNN now admits to this scientific fact. If the vaccines were truly effective, you wouldn't need to get a booster every six months. And you wouldn't worry about being in the same room with the unvaccinated.

2. "There is no *crisis* at the border." We have all seen video of thousands of illegal immigrants crowded under a bridge on the Texas border and millions more flooding our country. The states of Texas, Arizona, and others have filed lawsuits against Joe Biden because of the absolute insanity taking place at the American southern border. But yeah, there's no crisis at the border. Talk about gaslighting! And what's the deal with paying illegal immigrants separated from their families under the Trump administration $450,000 each. Yeah, that's a real thing! How about paying $450,000 to healthcare workers who lost their jobs because they wouldn't get the jab. Or to the families of AMERICANS who lost their son or daughter in the line of duty? I could go on.

3. "The withdrawal from Afghanistan was a huge success." I literally heard Jen Psaki in a press conference say the White House views the Afghanistan withdrawal as a major accomplishment and huge success. Never mind the thirteen American soldiers who lost their lives, images you saw of Afghans clinging desperately to military aircraft eventually falling to their death, or the billions of dollars' worth of military equipment we left behind for the Taliban to use. I wonder what a failed withdrawal would look like?

4. "The US economy and job market is doing better than it has in many years." Never mind inflation on everything from gas to groceries to energy costs this winter. Fact, inflation is higher than it has been in 40 years. And oh yeah, Biden said his Build Back Better bill was already paid for. This goes beyond gaslighting, it's just playing the American people for fools.

5. "Joe Biden is the president of unity and wants to stop the divisiveness in our country." Never mind he clearly said that anyone who voted for Trump isn't really black (probably the most racist comment ever uttered by a US President). Never mind he unashamedly supports a woman's right to choose, "My Body, My Choice." But at the same time is tyrannically dictating what gets injected into every BODY. Never mind he has made reference to Trump supporters as "white supremacists." Biden creates more division in one press conference than most presidents do in an entire four-year term.

It's like the mainstream media and Biden are trying to use some Jedi mind trick on us by waving their hand over our head telling us, "There's nothing to see here." When all the while what we are seeing is our country being dismantled beyond belief. An entire country has never been so gaslighted as it has over the first year of Biden's presidency. (Wait, I take that back. Justin Trudeau calling the trucker's convoy a "fringe movement" was just as bad.) And the vaccine has been the perfect tool to push the control and power buttons to a new level. We used to be able to trust the government, mainstream media, and government agencies like the CDC, FDA, and FBI, and the DOJ. Those days are long gone.

"Let's Go Brandon" means much more than "F... Joe Biden." It's symbolic of a sinister agenda to convince the American people that we are not seeing what we are seeing or hearing what we are hearing. Thank you, NASCAR and NBC reporter Kelli Stavast for the wonderfully illuminating interview that showed the American public how gaslighting really works. Oh yeah, and thank you, Brandon Brown, for winning Talladega in October! Your win and your name helped expose mainstream media as perverse gaslighters.

A final note on mainstream media, specifically CNN. You know by now Chris Cuomo, brother to Andrew Cuomo, was fired for trying to help his brother ward off charges of sexual misconduct. But it runs much deeper than that. By now you have also probably heard about the producer who worked hand-in-hand with Chris Cuomo. Here's what the *New York Post* had to say: "A veteran CNN producer who worked 'shoulder to shoulder' with now disgraced ex-anchor Chris Cuomo has been indicted on charges of luring young girls to his Vermont ski house for 'sexual subservience training.'" CNN is going to have a lot more problems than their plummeting ratings in the months to come.

If you have one of the main anchors for CNN, Chris Cuomo, trying to help his brother get away with sexual assault, why would you invite him into your living room each night and entrust him with reporting the truth? And his producer, doing such things as luring young girls in for "sexual subservience training," why would you entrust him to bring you an honest nightly news feed? (Even the untouchable Don Lemon now has allegations swirling around him.) These are not trustworthy characters. This is not a trustworthy network. If you are still watching CNN, you are watching news produced and told by lying, cheating pedophiles. Uh . . . I wonder if they could also be covering up hard truth regarding the safety of the vaccines? If you've never asked that question, it's obviously a good time to start.

CNN surely didn't air Dr. Fauci's interview on Facebook with Mark Zuckerberg on March 26, 2020, where Fauci actually states, "The vaccine could make things worse." Might want to check that one out. They also didn't air Fauci stating, "Masks don't work against such small particles that make up the virus." Yep, he actually said that and then a few months later stated two masks aren't such a bad idea. I have never heard CNN once call him out for those gross inconsistencies.

CNN is not journalism; it is diabolical deception. CNN, the Communist News Network, had a good run, but it's over now. If you watch other news networks and view other media outlets that aren't just another branch of the Democratic party, you know we have been gaslit, and gaslit hard!

America is catching on, and CNN's viewership has never plummeted so hard so fast. And other mainstream media is right behind them. If you don't think you have been severely lied to, then try watching other news outlets like Newsmax or Real America's Voice for a week. There are two distinct realities going on in America right now. One is the truth and the other is a lie. It's quite challenging to discern between the two. But maybe it's not so hard after all? Maybe if we just listen, we will hear the crowd isn't really chanting, "Let's Go Brandon."

CHAPTER 11

My Body, My Choice

> I was eight months pregnant, but I was still required to get the
> vaccine or I would be fired in two weeks. I told the HR guy
> if anything happened to my baby I would sue them. The HR
> "advocate" responded, 'Go right ahead, we're ready.'
> **—Colleague**

She had just bought a house and was about to have her first baby. She told HR, "I will get the vaccine AFTER I have my baby." She was even willing to sign an affidavit documenting her promise. Well, HR said she had to get the Covid vaccine or be fired in two weeks. What a hell of a choice! This vaccine is so new, who knows what will happen to babies in utero? But she felt she had no choice. So she told HR, "If anything happens to my baby, I will sue you." HR responded, "Go right ahead, we're ready." I guess "My Body, My Choice" only applies if you choose to murder your baby, not keep it!

"My Body, My Choice" is a phrase we have all heard related to a women's right to get an abortion. This phrase has been shouted from the rooftops at rallies, in courtrooms, and in mainstream media. We all know that a woman has a protected legal right to kill the baby living inside her womb. I vehemently disagree with this legal decision, but the courts have decided a woman can do whatever she wants with her body, including ripping a living being out of it.

Now, when we say "My Body, My Choice" related to the vaccine, this same freedom doesn't apply. And if you are on the left don't use the argument that a woman getting an abortion is not hurting society, but someone who doesn't get the vaccine is. That kind of logic is not only idiotic, but also extremely dangerous.

A woman who gets an abortion snuffs out life, a person who doesn't get a vaccine is simply not getting a chemical put in their body. The comparison shouldn't be uttered in the same breath. The same crowd vehemently chanting, "My Body, My Choice," is now trying to deny the rights of those who choose not to put a chemical in their body. This is hypocrisy at its finest, and a most ironic double-standard.

How does "my body, my choice" relate to vaccine exemptions? It's a fair question. After all, putting an experimental drug into your body is a significant choice related to the mantra, "my body, my choice." It's obviously not near as critical a choice as destroying the baby inside of you, but still a very crucial choice for one's own health and well-being. If one set of beliefs is protected under the law, why not the other? Especially since the protected belief is much more extreme and life altering.

As you have probably heard, there are two types of exemptions people are applying for. One is getting a medical exemption because of a previous underlying medical condition the vaccine could exacerbate. The other is getting a religious exemption because of sincerely held religious beliefs that prevent a person from taking a drug or medication which would violate their conscience. I applied for both because I had no clue how my company would respond to either.

Religious Exemption

I shared at the outset that I minored in Biblical Studies at the Christian University I attended. I definitely had this documentation ready for my interview with HR. In preparation for this interview, I had to gather a few other pieces of information proving my religious beliefs were legitimate, and not a false claim.

One of the things I had to provide was a letter from my pastor. The letter my pastor wrote my company said, "He is not only a member of our church, but also a valued leader. He has served in multiple volunteer leadership roles and is an integral part of our body of believers. He is also an honest and wonderful Christian who seeks to honor God with his life. How he takes care of his body is part of honoring God. And his refrain from taking the vaccines is done from a sincere conscience." I was thankful for the kind words my pastor wrote. With my minor in Biblical studies from a Christian University, my leadership roles within the church, and this letter I felt I had a very good chance of getting a religious exemption.

The first thing I did in my HR interview was share Bible verses from memory that I felt very passionate about. I started by sharing what the apostle Paul said about not going against your own conscience. "Holding on to faith and a good **conscience**, which some have rejected and so have suffered shipwreck with regard to the faith" (1 Timothy 1:19, NIV). I also shared 1 Timothy 3:9 which states, "They must keep hold of the deep truths of the faith with a clear **conscience**" (NIV). I explained the importance of doing things with a clear conscience. And for me personally, I would be violating my own conscience if I took the vaccine.

Secondly, we discussed the Biblical importance of honoring and caring for one's own body. "Do you not know that your body is the temple of the Holy Spirit, who is in you, whom you have received from God? You are not your own, you were bought at a price. Therefore, honor God with your body" (1 Corinthians 6:19-20 NIV). I shared the importance of caring for the body God has given me. I talked about foods I eat and don't eat. I don't drink alcohol. And I very rarely take any medications that could harm the body God has given me. I also shared details of my work-out schedule and how diligent I am when it comes to taking care of the body God has given me. I view my life as a gift from God, and taking care of my body is an integral part of my faith. (I am one of those guys who competes in triathlons, just for fun!)

Lastly, I shared scripture that backed up my pro-life stance. This relates specifically to refraining from taking certain medications, like the Covid vaccines, which used fetal cell lines for their development. Here is why I believe so strongly in the sanctity of life, "For you created my inmost being; you knit me together in my mother's womb. I praise you because I am fearfully and wonderfully made; your works are wonderful; I know that full well" (Psalm 139:13-14 NIV). I believe life begins at conception in the womb, period. And I will not take part in anything that destroys the gift of life given to us by our Creator.

On a personal note; my mother was extremely close to getting an abortion with me. If she had lived in San Francisco at the time she was pregnant with me, she would have definitely gone through with the abortion. At that time, bigger cities like San Francisco and New York City were some of the only places with abortion clinics. Pro-abortion clinics were not near as prevalent as they are today. She lived out in the country, and San Fran was the nearest city with an abortion clinic. She had no money and no car. So even a five-hour drive wasn't feasible for her. Getting an abortion back then wasn't nearly as convenient as it is today. I have heard the phrase, "convenience kills." In this case it literally would have. I am so glad it wasn't as convenient then as it is now!

The HR person doing my interview gave me the vibe that it didn't matter what my education, background, or service in the church was. She was not giving me a religious exemption. Because of the negative tone I got from her, I decided to also apply for a medical exemption. I told my wife about the interview and negative feel I got from this HR lady. My wife assured me I would get the religious exemption because of my education from a Christian University, documented leadership roles within our church, and an encouraging letter from our pastor. She thought it was a waste of time to go through all the trouble of submitting a medical exemption. And she was probably right. But I still had that gnawing feeling in my gut this HR lady wasn't going to grant me the exemption. Well, I didn't listen to my wife on this one. I applied for the medical exemption. I just didn't feel this HR "advocate" was really advocating for me.

Fast-forward a month, and I'm glad I applied for the medical exemption, because I did not get the religious exemption. Friends and family that know my education, background, and leadership in our church were shocked I did not get the exemption. I was a bit surprised myself.

When a few of my colleagues, who also did not get a religious exemption, heard I did not get it, they asked me to join their lawsuit. We have since learned our company hasn't granted one religious exemption. I was fine with submitting my pastor's letter, documenting my service in the church, and having an open discussion with this HR lady about my religious convictions as it relates to the vaccine. But what I'm not ok with is our company not granting even one religious exemption.

What boils my blood is that my company collected all of our personal religious beliefs knowing full-well they weren't giving out any religious exemptions. Either give out religious exemptions to those who show good faith, or don't collect any of our private religious convictions. I have never been a lawsuit type of guy. But if my company keeps pushing, I will most certainly do what I have to do to protect myself and our Constitutional freedoms.

Think about this for a second: Our company's insurance benefit actually pays for an employee to undergo hormone replacement therapy and/ or get a sex change. But the benefit doesn't stop there. Travel and lodging are also provided for anyone in my company who chooses to get a sex change. This is all part of the new corporate religion called DEI: Diversity, Equity, and Inclusion. (A discussion for another time.) However, my company is making me get an experimental drug shot into my arm even though I don't believe it's right. They are supporting a transgender's belief to completely malign and mangle their body. While at the same time telling me my beliefs regarding my body are not valid. This sounds a lot more like discrimination than inclusion? My company, and many across our great land, are supporting the beliefs of one group while clearly denying the religious freedoms of another. The inequality of this nonsense is absolute absurdity. And companies will be held accountable once people wake up from their wokeness.

Medical Exemption

I have a medical condition that precludes me from getting the vaccine. It's something I have dealt with my entire life. And it's well documented by previous testing and lab work. At times my bloodwork has been off the charts scary. Subsequently, my physician orders bloodwork every year to make sure everything is in normal range. I have to be extremely vigilant about taking care of my health because of my particular condition. My physician has me on a medication, vitamins, and a multitude of lifestyle modifications to counter my debilitating condition. If I adhere to his recommendations, I'm good. If I don't, I go downhill fast.

When I applied for the exemption, I provided all my personal medical records related to my condition. This spanned some years, so it was no small task to gather all the official copies and paperwork. I submitted my original diagnosis from years ago. I also submitted my bloodwork that verified my diagnosis and informed my treatment plan. Furthermore, l provided statements from my personal physician affirming it would be dangerous to my health to get the vaccine because it would most certainly aggravate my pre-existing condition.

Even after submitting documentation regarding a medical condition I have been dealing with for years, and after my personal physician of many years stated the vaccine could exasperate my condition, this HR "advocate" still interrogated me with questions about the validity of my condition. She had the nerve to ask me if my condition was "really that serious." I wanted to let her have it. But I also realized she played an important role in deciding my exemption. So, I reluctantly refrained from giving her more truth than she could handle.

The other maddening thing about the interrogation was when she asked me if I had talked to anyone who knew the specifics about my condition related to the vaccine. I responded with some attitude, "I didn't talk to just anyone, I talked to **my personal physician** of many years who knows everything about my condition. That's who I talked to." Again, I could have said much more in response, but getting angry with her wouldn't have helped my case.

The entire feel of the conversation, or more like interrogation, was her trying to trip me up. She was not looking out for my personal health. She was trying to get me to say something incriminating so as not to give me a medical exemption. I found this absolutely hypocritical when looking back at the depths our company has gone to make the medications we sell safe for the consumer. As previously stated, our company changed the name of a drug we launched and then spent millions of dollars remarketing the newly named drug for the safety of the consumer. They sure weren't taking the same approach with me and my medical safety.

How about doing the right thing for their employees? Here I am, a valued employee, or maybe not so much, who has worked for this company for seventeen years. They don't care two cents about my health and the potential harm a vaccine could do to me.

The interrogation continued. She was poking and attacking, and I was defending. The one time I did go on the offensive is when she said condescendingly, "I know this is difficult, but we are just following the mandate from the White House." (Our company put out their own vaccine mandate one week after Biden announced that companies over 100 employees mandate vaccination OR weekly testing.) I told her, "No, you're not following the mandate. You're going one step beyond. Biden said get vaccinated *or* get weekly testing. What happened to the testing option?" She didn't really answer. But yet I am put in a position where I have to answer very probing medical questions regarding my personal health, which, by the way, is a violation of HIPPA.

The last question she asked me was, "What do you want your exemption to look like?" I told her I wanted to continue to get weekly testing so

I could go out in the field and do my job. Before the mandate, the entire sales force underwent weekly testing and went out in the field. I simply asked for this weekly testing procedure to continue, nothing new.

Fast-forward a month, and I did, in fact, get a medical exemption. But here's the catch. The exemption is only good for three months. Then they will re-evaluate. My medical condition is not going to change. It is a lifelong illness. I don't know what they're going to re-evaluate? The other crazy thing about my exemption is I am only able to work remotely. Yeah, you heard that right. Even though they granted me a three-month medical exemption, they're not allowing me to get weekly testing and go out into the field, even though the unvaccinated and vaccinated alike can spread Covid. I reminded the HR lady of this scientific FACT when she gave me the verdict.

The mandates are all about optics, not people's health and well-being. If it was truly about our safety, these vaccines would have been pulled from the market months ago because of the millions of adverse events and simply because they don't work. Remember, if all this was really about our health as a nation, our southern border wouldn't be wide open. Millions of UNVACCINATED illegal immigrants wouldn't be flooding into our country every single day. Tell you what, when our government mandates vaccines for EVERY illegal coming across the border, then I will consider getting vaccinated.

Here's the absurdity of it all: American businesses and large HCOs are firing healthcare workers who don't get vaccinated, but allowing illegal immigrants to enter our cities unvaccinated. Figure that one out for me. Oh well, that's pretty easy considering the push for noncitizens being able to vote. Oh yeah, that's a reality now. A law permitting non-US citizens to vote was just passed in NYC. Obviously, these mandates are really all about power and control, not your health and safety.

PART III

The Way Forward

CHAPTER 12

Success

Plans fail for lack of counsel, but with many advisers they succeed.
—Proverbs 15:22 (NIV)

A lot has changed and will continue to change related to the pandemic, COVID-19, and the vaccines. But one thing that hasn't changed is the constant gaslighting that has gone on related to the vaccine safety and efficacy. We clearly see the vaccines aren't working. Omicron ripping through both unvaccinated and vaccinated alike is clear evidence of the lack of vaccine efficacy. Recently, even Pfizer's CEO Albert Bourla admitted to this. Also, if the COVID vaccines really worked, would the vaccinated still be afraid to be in the same room with the unvaccinated? And just look at the dismal VAERS data. It's downright frightening to see the number of deaths and serious adverse events that have been reported after taking the COVID vaccines.

What we have witnessed over the last two years has been unprecedented, to say the least. It has been a turbulent time for everyone in the entire world, not just in our little corner of the globe. As time goes by, it will be interesting to see what truths continue to emerge. People who are now vilified by mainstream media will be exonerated. And those whom mainstream media touts as heroes may wind up in jail.

Facts like the virus being deliberately manufactured from a lab in Wuhan and then purposely unleashed on the world by China were once considered sheer absurdity and wild conspiracy theory. If you even whispered such a statement you were considered to be spewing misinformation. Now this has come to be known as common fact.

If you previously dared question Science himself, Anthony Fauci, and the legitimacy of the vaccines, you were labeled as a rabid white supremist, one of those crazy Trump supporters. You were considered a selfish, evil scourge against society if unvaccinated, because you deliberately were spreading Covid. As Biden said, "This is a pandemic of the unvaccinated."

The hard truth is, the vaccines simply don't work. If they did, the vaccinated wouldn't have to worry about being in the same room with the unvaccinated. If the vaccines worked, Omicron would not be so rampant in society. And if they truly worked, the CEO of Pfizer wouldn't have said, "the two doses, they're not enough for Omicron."

Now you can raise a question about the safety of the vaccines without being called an enemy of the state. Well, maybe you will still be labeled a scourge on society. It's still a pretty big offense if you question one of the biggest lies ever perpetrated on civilization. But trying to get to the truth by asking questions and engaging in healthy debate is worth it. Free speech good, communism bad!

Change is the only thing permanent. This will hold especially true over the next few years related to COVID-19 and the vaccines. The changes don't just happen every month, but seemingly every day. And sometimes true scientific knowledge does come to the forefront related to Covid-19 and the vaccines. But too often the scientific goalposts keep changing to accommodate a political agenda. This is what has gotten us into trouble. Politicizing the pandemic has not helped us to get out of it.

We all want success. We all want to end this pandemic and get on with our lives. So, what is our way forward? How can we win over COVID-19? The first step is to realize we need more than one or two voices illuminating the way. We have depended far too long on this one-size-fits-all narrative propagated by Big Pharma and Big Government with one man, Anthony Fauci, as their mouthpiece. "Plans fail for lack of counsel, but with many advisers they succeed" (Proverbs 15:22 NIV).

As mentioned in chapter 4, we desperately need to get a second opinion. There are many renowned experts in the field of infectious disease and virology that Senator Ron Johnson brought together on January 24, 2022. For five hours they discussed what's gone right, what's gone wrong, and our best way forward. And this expert panel discussion is available for all to view. No censorship here. Nothing to hide. A dozen of the most successful physicians in our country showed up for this roundtable. Of course, this was banned on YouTube and other outlets that only allow one narrative.

If you are serious about getting to the truth of the matter at hand, which is getting out of this pandemic, then watch the symposium. None of these physicians are getting paid to promote the vaccine—so they just might be a little more trustworthy than those getting incentivized by Big Pharma. And, by the way, the physicians are a bi-partisan panel.

I have three suggestions to help us find our way out of the pandemic. Instead of being VAXLIT, let's open our eyes and ears and come back to reality. I just listed the first suggestion. Watch the "Second Opinion" symposium on Rumble. It's truly enlightening and offers us an illuminated path out of COVID darkness. My wife, who never swears, exclaimed "Oh shit" after watching the blatant malpractice of the pandemic be exposed.

My second suggestion is to watch Joe Rogan's podcast with Dr. Peter McCullough. Dr. Peter McCullough was one of the first physicians in the nation to develop early treatment protocols to beat COVID. And he was successful. He is one of the most published cardiologists of all time. He has over 650 Pub-Med listings. This doc is legit! He is not getting paid or endorsed to say what he says. In fact, he's taken a tremendous amount of heat from his workplace, Baylor University Medical Center, because he called out the inconsistencies and absurdities of how we are treating COVID-19. (Universities get extra funding to go along with the vaccine narrative. That's why they get so touchy, even when one of their superstars speak out.)

My final suggestion, if you haven't already, is to watch Joe Rogan's podcast with the inventor of mRNA technology. The COVID-19 vaccines wouldn't exist without him. Dr. Robert Malone's research and life's work has been developing safe and effective vaccines to help society. He is the most pro-vaccine doctor on the planet. However, mainstream media paints him as this rebel doctor who's out to deceive the general public. Nothing could be further from the truth. If you don't believe me, watch him for yourself. Make your own opinion. Don't just listen to CNN. After all the deception they have been exposed for over the last couple years, why would you give them anymore of your precious time?

Take your pick from any of these three suggestions. You will see after watching, these physicians are humble, compassionate, and courageously arguing for truth and a legitimate way out of the pandemic. Their goal is the same as yours: to win over COVID-19.

Their goal is not money, power, and control. They are worth being listened to. They are truly worth a second opinion.

Bringing both sides together for healthy debate will guide us to success, a true way out. Squelching any information contrary to Big Pharma and Big Government's tyrannical mantra demanding everyone "must be vaccinated or else" has not helped. We are still knee-deep in it. If we want success, if we want a way out, we must listen to many advisers, not just one man audaciously claiming to be science himself.

We have all heard the one-size-fits-all vaccine narrative ad nauseam. Enough vaxlighting! It's time to hear the other side. It's time for a second opinion. Then you can make an informed choice. Then you can decide for yourself which route is the best way out of the COVID-19 pandemic.

"Plans fail for lack of counsel, but with many advisers they succeed" (Proverbs 15:22 NIV).

Good luck to us all!

Made in the USA
Columbia, SC
01 March 2022

56555807R00067